tell B
£5.
10
to pay the Bearer
VE POUNDS, Value receive
ay of Jany 1819 No. 185
Ball, Hamilton & Co.

BRITISH BAN

BRITISH BANKS AND BANKING

a pictorial history

R. M. FITZMAURICE

F.C.I.S., ASSOCIATE OF THE INSTITUTE OF BANKERS

D. BRADFORD BARTON LIMITED

FRONTISPIECE. **A Silver Inkstand**—Despite strong competition between the banks, there remain many matters on which there must be consultation and agreement. This is symbolised by this beautiful example of the modern silversmith's art. Presented by the Bank of England to mark the completion of a new Committee Room for the London Clearing Bankers in 1958, it is ornamented by the medallions of the Bank of England, and each of the then Clearing Banks. The badges to be seen from left to right are Glyn Mills & Co, Bank of England, National, Barclays and District Banks. However, with the amalgamations of recent years only the Bank of England and Barclays still have an independent existence.

 ISBN 0 85153 154 7
printed in Great Britain by H. E. Warne Ltd, London and St. Austell
for the publishers

D. BRADFORD BARTON LTD · Trethellan House · Truro · Cornwall

introduction

Although banking, as we know it, has its roots in the seventeenth century, many of its features can be traced to ancient times. In the Roman Empire an extensive international trade demanded banking facilities—the lending of money—its exchange for foreign trade and travel—and the safe keeping of deposits.

An English village community in mediaeval times—organised within the feudal system and largely self-sufficient—had no need for banking but for merchants in the growing towns, trading both at home and abroad, a knowledge of money became essential.

Kings and great lords anticipated their revenues to buy luxuries, often from abroad, or raise armies for war. Since the Christian Church forbad the lending of money for interest, Jewish immigrants to England—barred from ordinary trade, living frugally and not bound by the Church's laws—filled the need for money lenders.

The Jews were banished in the thirteenth century leaving a vacuum which was filled by merchants from the great trading ports of northern Italy. They used methods which—with the name of Lombard Street in the heart of the London financial quarter—have survived to give our vocabulary 'cash', 'debtor', 'creditor' and 'ledger'. Their cryptic letters £.s.d. are only partly discarded on decimalisation.

As feudalism waned, trade increased and the manufacture of cloth and its export needed an efficient system to settle debts without the risks of shipping coin across the seas.

The sixteenth century, an age of discovery, and in England a long period of stable government under the Tudors, saw expansion of trade at home and abroad. Moreover, the Reformation swept through northern Europe and Henry VIII at the end of his reign partly repealed the Usury Laws—an act carried a stage further by his daughter Elizabeth. A scene was being set in which the foundations of the modern banking system could emerge.

Perhaps Sir Thomas Gresham, builder of the first Royal Exchange and financial agent to four Tudor monarchs, had some part in the change. Certainly he was quick to use Henry's new law, for in 1546 he advanced money "upon interest according to the King's Majesty's statute at ten per cent".

It is from the time of Gresham that this book tells the story and marks the development of banking in Britain. Since a span of almost 400 years of history has to be condensed into this volume there has been need for selection. Banking is a trade which keeps its records in print rather than picture and with a traditional secrecy destroys them when no longer of use. The salvage drives of two world wars and the fact that the camera did not appear until three quarters of the period had passed has meant that the material from which a selection can be made is somewhat limited.

Passing from the Tudor "Money Men" through the early seventeenth century there is little to record but by the time of the Commonwealth a banking system was appearing in the hands of the London goldsmiths not only recognisable in modern terms but connected by direct descent to some of the great commercial banks of our own day.

The Goldsmiths' business was a mixture of gold and silver smithery, dealing in precious stones, money changing, pawn broking and true banking. They would remit funds and hold deposits which they found they could lend along with their own money. Orders were drawn on them for payment resembling the modern cheque. They commenced to issue promissory notes which were the forerunners of the bank notes and which came to form an important part of the business of the banker in England for the next 250 years and in Scotland to this day.

In 1694, born of necessity in the war with France, came the foundation of the Bank of England. This had a Charter with a limited life of only twelve years although this was renewed successively down to nationalisation in 1946. In its early period the Bank of England had none of the monopoly of later times. It struggled successfully through a decade of open competition with its rivals until in 1708 the government of the day, in return for further financial support, prohibited the issue of notes in England by any banking firm of more than six partners.

Since the right to issue notes was considered essential to any bank, the 1708 "Monopoly" Act set a pattern of banking in England for more than a hundred years—and one which had many disadvantages. In practice no large scale bank with a network of branches could develop south of the Tweed.

The 1708 Act never applied to Scotland where the Bank of Scotland was formed soon after its English counterpart, before the 1707 Act of Union, under Scots Law. The Bank of Scotland had few special privileges and banking developed in Scotland in a rational way, by the large joint stock company with many branches. Foundation of the Bank of Scotland in 1696 was followed by the Royal Bank of Scotland in 1727 and the British Linen Bank in 1746.

In England the restrictions gave rise to the 'country banker', a small partnership with all the advantages of a close knowledge of local affairs but often with inadequate resources. Many of these small banks met disaster in successive crises. Others survived to become part of the modern banking system and in one case—Lloyds—gave its name to one of the great modern banks.

It was not until after 1750 that 'country bankers' existed to any extent but with the rising prosperity of the industrial revolution they multiplied from a dozen in that year to almost 800 in 1810. Side by side with the country bankers and the Bank of England, the London goldsmith bankers prospered, dropping their non-banking activities in the early 1700's. Joined by new firms they tended to specialise, providing commercial finance from the City and the needs of the aristocracy from Fleet Street and the Strand. From these London banks we trace the ancestry of the present-day merchant banks, with others becoming part of the modern banking system and in the name of Barclay showing a proud descent to the twentieth century.

At the low tide of war against France in 1797, with the Fleet in mutiny and public confidence sapped, many banks closed their doors. The reserves of the Bank of England were so depleted by loans to the Government and other calls that authority had to be given by Act of Parliament to stop payment of gold in exchange for Bank notes, a situation which lasted until 1821.

By the 1820's the Bank of England monopoly had outlived its usefulness. Whilst the formation of strongly based banks was prevented, any butcher, baker or candlestick maker could issue his own notes and call himself banker. A major crisis in banking in late 1825 and early 1826, which saw the failure of 60 banks, brought home the need for reform.

The Government took action and Acts in 1826 and 1833 allowed the formation of strong joint stock banks with numerous shareholders and networks of branches. This period saw the foundation of the National Provincial Bank of England, the London and Westminster as well as the Birmingham and Midland. All of these are names which survive only a little changed today. The Acts encouraged the Bank of England to expand outside London in commercial competition with the new joint stock banks, and the various Bank of England branches in provincial towns date from this period. This phase has long since passed and the Bank's branches now rovide banking services for the government and the rest of the banking community.

During the nineteenth century the techniques of banking progressed in many ways. The Clearing House, founded in London in 1770, to enable member banks to exchange each others cheques, grew steadily towards the organisation which in the 1970's can handle over 3,000,000 cheques with a value of more than £4,000 million in a single day.

Scotland weathered the difficulties of the early nineteenth century with her banks expanding in size and number into the twentieth century. Consolidation came later and the decades following the Second World War saw a final series of amalgamations with a return to the eighteenth century pattern of three large banks. We see the survival of the two original banks, the Bank of Scotland and the Royal Bank, now joined by the Clydesdale founded in 1838. Although Scottish banking pursues its own course a substantial financial interest is held by English banks and a reverse position exists with the National and Commercial Group

(Royal Bank) controlling the long established Glyn Mills and Williams Deacon's Banks.

In England, the latter part of the nineteenth century saw a period of amalgamations which accelerated in the early 1900's, until a final round just after the First World War brought together the "Big Five". These banks, each with several thousand branches, remained virtually unchanged in name and relative size for fifty years. The mergers which took place in the late 1960's produced a "Big Four" which with Williams & Glyn's, now cover the major part of the English commercial banking sector.

This country has had a stable banking system for the last hundred years and during this time London has in many ways been the financial centre of the world. Banking and the banks themselves are constantly changing yet we can still find that many of the services they give are recognisable in descent from the goldsmith bankers, the Tudor "Money Men" and the Lombards of the thirteenth century.

foreword

Finding suitable illustrations for this pictorial history would have been an impossible task had it not been for the assistance of the Institute of Bankers, the Bank of England, C. Hoare & Co., the English Clearing and Scottish Banks and other people and organisations. I acknowledge their kindness and list the items individually below.

Mr. Eric Kelly of the Bank of England not only met my every request but has kindly read and corrected the Bank of England Token Money caption. Miss Kathleen Bryon gave me the benefit of her unrivalled knowledge of the "Grasshopper" archives of the former Martins Bank as well as further assistance from the Barclays Bank records. Miss J. M. R. Campbell was most helpful in regard to the combined National Westminster Bank archives. Mr. F. Maslen assisted me in my search of the Lloyds Bank Museum material and in assembling the items I required. Miss Rosemary Ashbee, who has the care of the Williams & Glyn's archives and those of Child & Co., made most helpful suggestions, some of which are represented in this book. Miss M. V. Stokes, in a difficult period when Coutts and Co. were rebuilding their premises, found time to answer my queries and make available a number of illustrations.

I owe a debt to my colleagues, Mr. George Copeman and Mr. Ron Smith for their painstaking photographic work. I am grateful to Mr. Peter Spiro for his encouragement of the idea of an illustrated history and for permission to draw on the incomparable collection of English country bank notes at the Institute of Bankers Library. I have been guided through this collection by Mrs. J. M. Saunders who has gone to considerable trouble in arranging photography of the Institute material and other items in London. I have been fortunate in being allowed to reproduce several of the specially commissioned paintings of historical banking scenes which appeared in the Midland Bank 1971 calendar.

Wimborne, Dorset — R.M.F.

acknowledgements

Bank of England, 18, 19, 20, 21, 22, 23, 24, 34, 35, 36, 37, 38, 43, 53, 54, 55, 57, 58, 66, 67, 68, 93, 97, 101, 111, 113, 114, 125.
Bank of Scotland, 25, 26, 27, 50, 117.
Barclays Bank, 33, 61, 63, 65, 81, 109, 112, 120.
Barclays Bank (Martin's Collection), 3, 4, 5, 6, 7, 17, 59, 74, 86, 87.
Barrington, R., 91.
Bristol City Art Gallery, 88.
City of London Police, 107.
Committee of London Clearing Bankers, 127.
Coutts & Co., 72, 73.
Gresham Committee (Mercer's Hall), 1.
Hoare, C. & Co., 13.
Institute of Bankers, 47, 62, 69, 78, 80, 83, 85, 110.
Leicester Museum, 84.
Lloyds Bank, 44, 45, 46, 89, 92, 123, 126.
Mercers' Company, 2.
Metropolitan Police, 94.
Midland Bank, 12, 28, 51, 56, 96, 104, 106, 108, 118, 119, 121, 122, 124.
National Westminster Bank, 10, 11, 40, 41, 42, 48, 52, 90, 95, 102, 103, 115.
Overbury Court Archives, 39.
Ridley, P., 82.
Royal Bank of Scotland, 49, 70, 71.
Royal Institution of Cornwall, 76, 77.
Vauxhall Motors, 123.
Williams & Glyn's Bank, 14, 15, 16, 31, 32, 105.

1. **Sir Thomas Gresham**—He has claim to be considered a "father of English banking" and was a pioneer of the lending and borrowing of money at interest in this country. He served Henry VIII, Edward VI, Queen Mary and Queen Elizabeth as royal financial agent. His portrait, attributed to the School of Holbein, shows something of the commanding personality which made him the "greatest merchant in London" and perhaps the most successful of the Tudor "Money Men". Drawn below his name is the merchant mark which appeared on every bale of goods passing through his warehouses.

2. **Gresham's Journal 1546-1552**—This account book begins from the year he started in business on his own account. In the margin can be seen his merchant mark and the number of each consignment of goods.

3. **The Grasshopper Ring**—Gresham used the badge of the grasshopper and by 1563 was carrying on large scale financial transactions from Lombard Street premises displaying the sign. He presented a number of rings to prominent people when the first Royal Exchange, which he built, was opened by Queen Elizabeth in 1571.

4. **Grasshopper Sign**—Originally gilded, this is believed to be the replacement of the first sign displayed outside the premises of Sir Thomas Gresham in Lombard Street. The original sign was destroyed in the Great Fire of 1666.

5. **Letter of Queen Elizabeth to Sir Thomas Gresham**—This letter, signed on behalf of the Queen in 1567, authorises Gresham to pay one of her debts in Antwerp. With the worsening of relations with Philip of Spain, who controlled the Low Countries, borrowing there became impossible and she followed Gresham's advice to take up money from her own merchants.

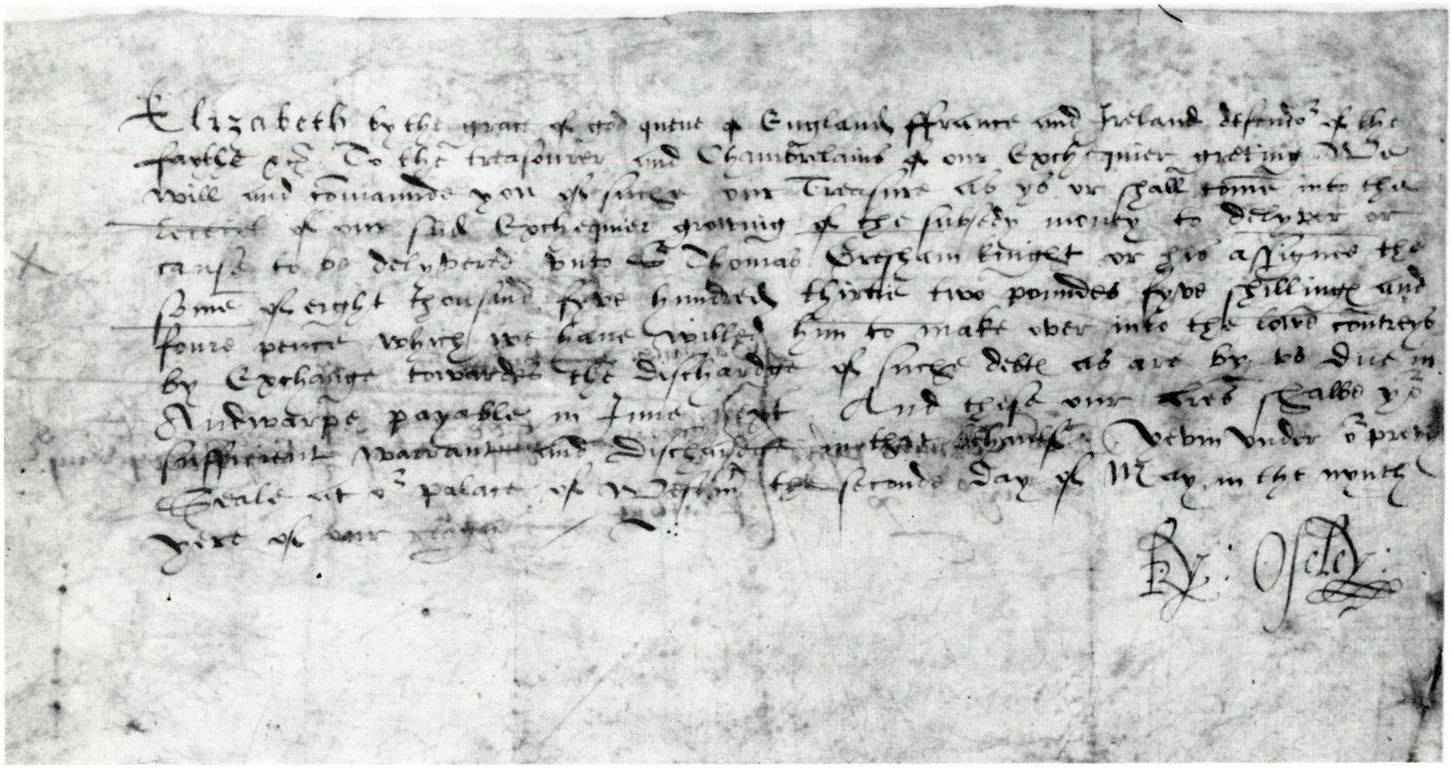

Elizabeth by the grace of god quene of England ffraunce and Ireland defendo[r] of the faithe &c. To the treasourer and Chamberlains of our Exchequier greting We will and commaunde you of suche our treasure as yo[u] or shall come into the receipt of our said Exchequier growing of the subsidy money to deliver or cause to be delivered unto Sr Thomas Gresham knight or his assignes the some of eight thousand five hundred thirtie two poundes fyve shillinge and foure pence which we have willed him to make over into the lowe countreys by Exchange towardes the discharge of suche debte as are by us due in Andwarpe payable in June next And these our lres shalbe yo[u]r sufficient warraunt and discharge in that behalf. Yeven under o[u]r privie Seale at o[u]r palaice of Westm the seconde day of May in the ninthe yere of our reigne.

By: Oseley

6. **Sir Richard Martin**—Goldsmith, money lender, bullion merchant, Warden of the Mint. At the Mint on 23 December 1580 Sir Francis Drake delivered to him 23,000 lbs of silver and 100 lbs of gold bullion. This would be part of the booty taken during the circumnavigation of the world completed by Drake the previous September. Martin was associated with Gresham both in raising money for the Queen and in a re-coinage of "Her Majesty's Money". Such craftsmen-goldsmiths and money-lenders were the forerunners of the goldsmith bankers of Stuart London from whom a number of the present day banks are directly descended.

7. **The Goldsmith's Shop**—This woodcut of an early Stuart Goldsmith's shop implies no popular esteem. The spoken words "I say I will have all both use (interest) and principal" and the representation of the Devil perched on the back of the chair suggest Englishmen had not come willingly to the idea of paying interest for a loan. The mediaeval Catholic church forbad interest payments. Queen Elizabeth partially repealed the Usury Laws in 1571 to allow interest at 10 per cent. This was reduced to 8 per cent in 1623, 6 per cent in 1660, 5 per cent in 1713 and the Usury Laws were not finally repealed until 1854.

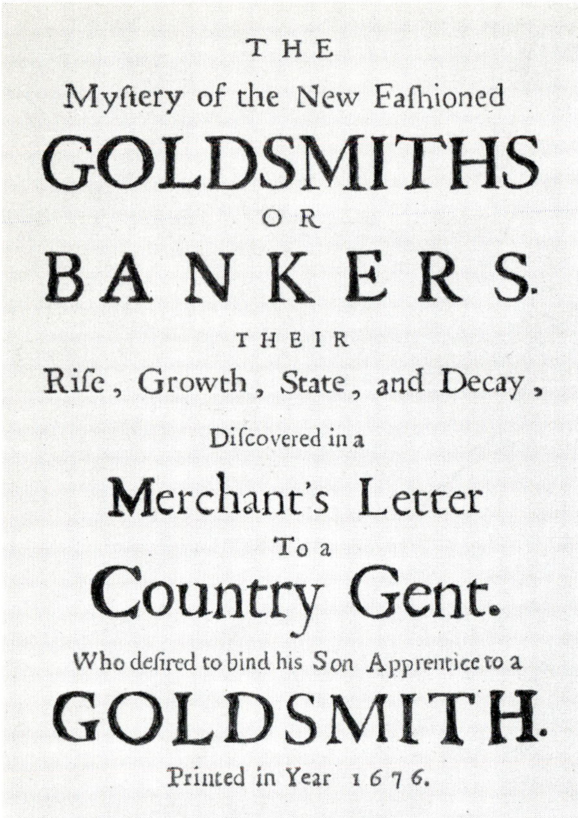
THE
Myſtery of the New Faſhioned
GOLDSMITHS
OR
BANKERS.
THEIR
Riſe, Growth, State, and Decay,
Diſcovered in a
Merchant's Letter
To a
Country Gent.
Who deſired to bind his Son Apprentice to a
GOLDSMITH.
Printed in Year 1676.

8. **The Stuart Goldsmith Bankers**—By the time of the Restoration of Charles II in 1660 a system of banking which we can recognise had emerged. Although the London goldsmith still carried on his traditional dealing in bullion, plate and jewels, to some a true banker's trade was becoming more important. Interest was paid on deposits, loans were given. Customers drew on their accounts by written authority to pay a third party (cheques). Promissory notes—direct forerunners of the printed bank notes—were widely used. No doubt all was revealed behind the quaintly worded title page of this pamphlet printed in 1676.

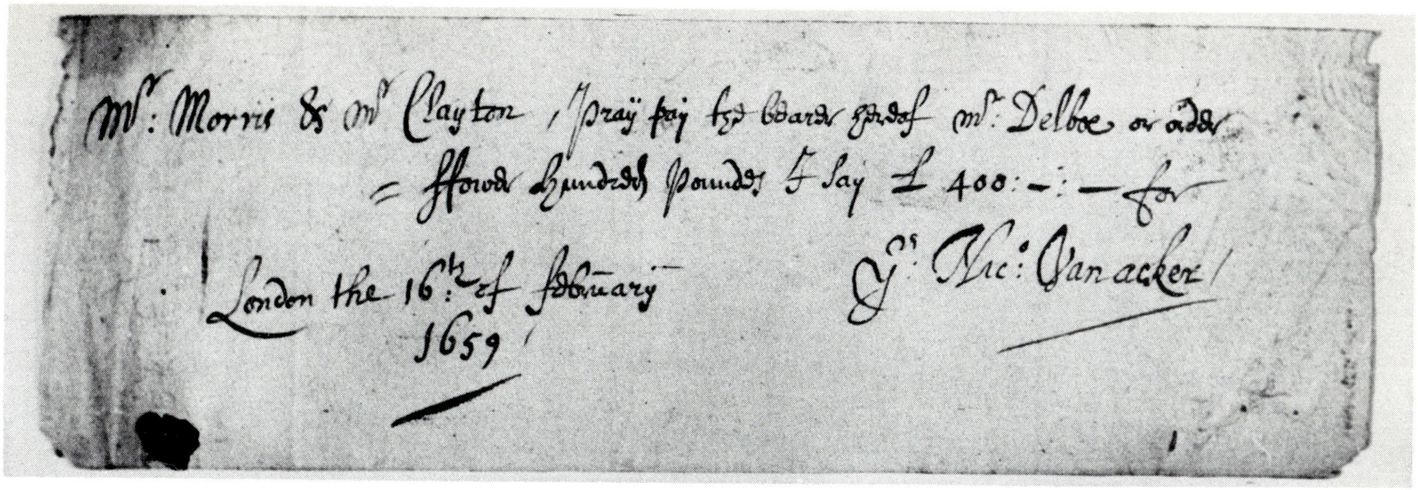

Mr: Morris & Mr Clayton, I pray pay to bearer hereof Mr: Delboe or order
= ffower hundred pounds & say £ 400:-:- for
London the 16th of February 1659
Yrs Nic: Vanacker

10. The earliest known English Cheque 1659—Clayton and Morris were scriveners, bankers and estate agents in Cornhill. More properly this should be known as a "drawn note" for the word "cheque" was not used until well into the next century.

9. The Goldsmiths' signs in Lombard Street—In an illiterate age an easily recognisable sign was essential to every tradesman. These signs were in use in the seventeenth and eighteenth centuries in Lombard Street on premises used by goldsmith bankers or their successors. Two of them—the Black Horse and the Spread Eagle—are badges of present day banks, Barclays and Lloyds.

11. Prescott's Balance—Although made in 1761 by Samuel Read, these scales, on which gold and silver were weighed are typical of those used by the London goldsmiths and their successors for 300 years. They are kept at the Cornhill office of Prescott & Co., now part of the National Westminster Bank.

12. **Pepys and Backwell**—Diary 5 June 1662—"To Alderman Backwell's to see some thousands of my Lord's crusados weighed, and we find the 3,000 comes to about £540 generally." Here we see the Alderman and his wife receiving the Diarist. Backwell was one of the greatest of the Stuart goldsmith bankers. He was banker to the Commonwealth and State and private banker to Charles II. He held accounts for customers from all parts of England. His account for the East India Company in 1671 showed receipts of £237,000—a considerable sum in an age when a maid servant had an annual wage of £4. He kept accounts on a very large scale for other London goldsmith bankers and with many foreign merchants.

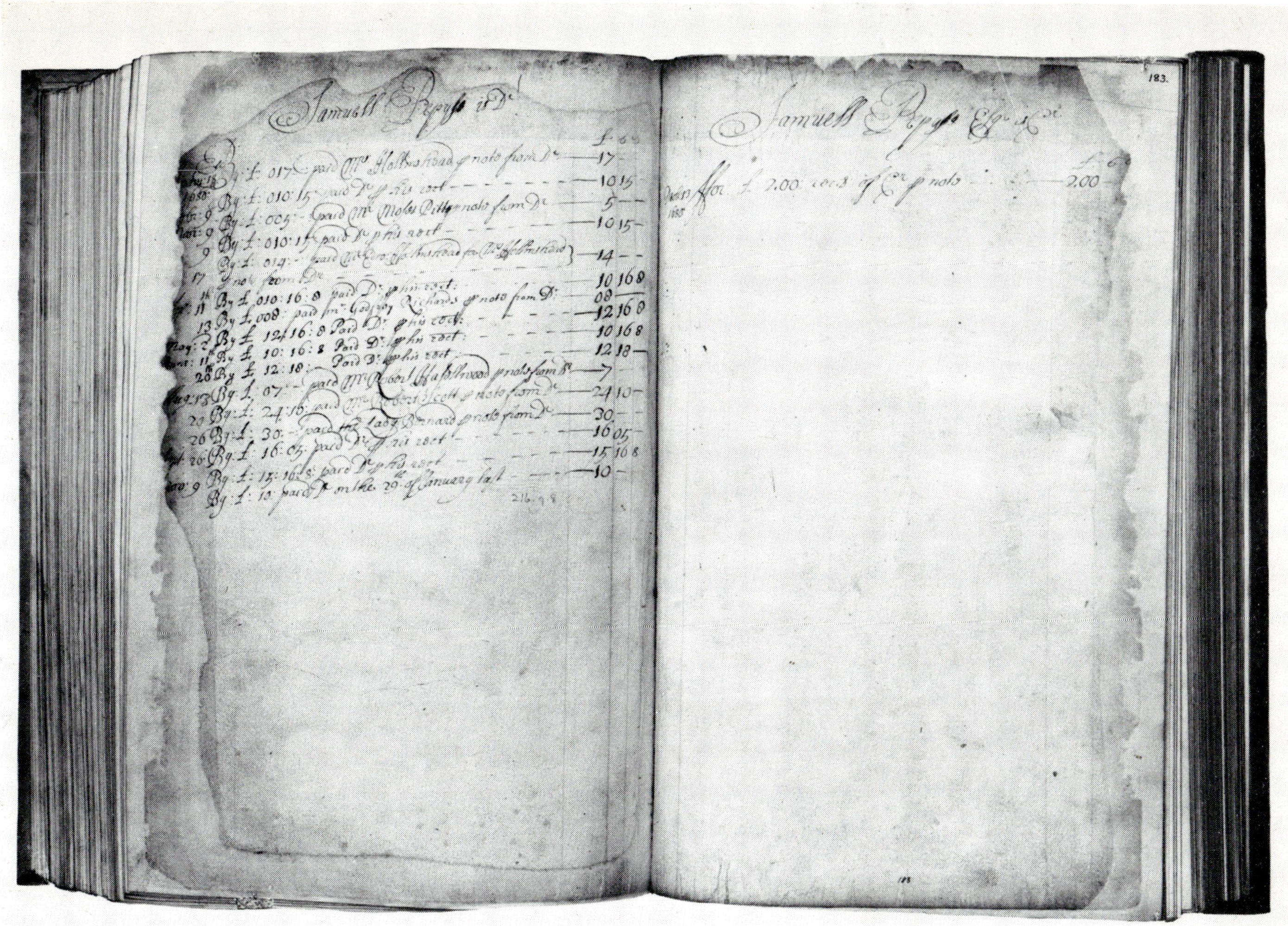

13. **Hoares' Ledger 1680**—From 1673 Richard Hoare traded as a goldsmith and banker at the sign of the Golden Bottle in Cheapside and from 1690 in Fleet Street. Hoares remain there to this day, a private bank controlled by the founding family. This ledger shows the account of Samuel Pepys who was numbered amongst their many well-known customers.

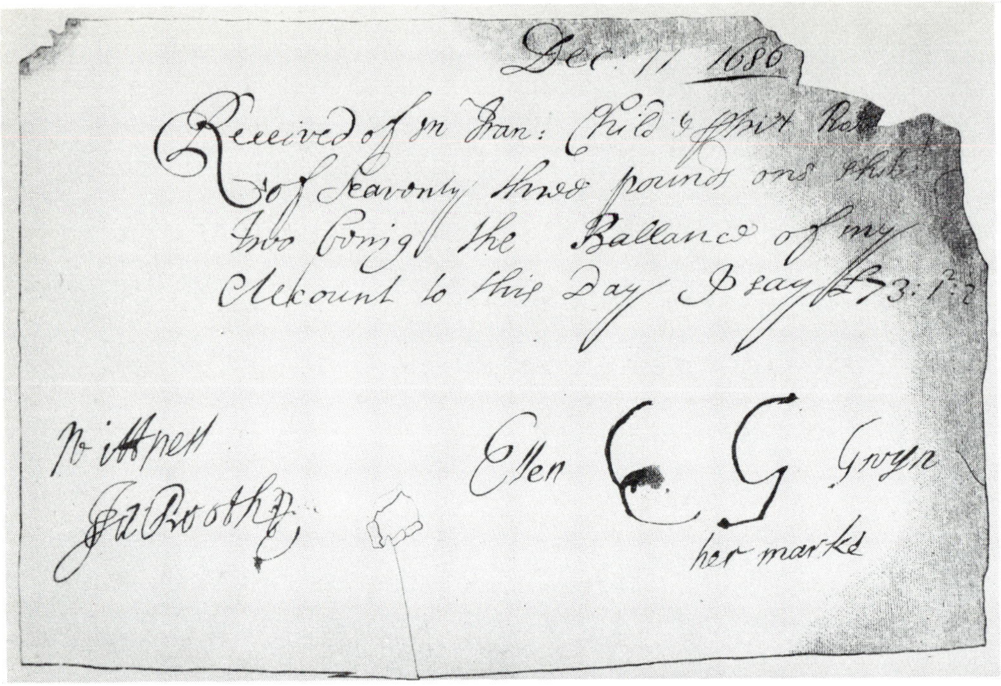
Dec. 17 1686
Received of Mr Fran: Child & [illegible]
of seavonty three pounds one shil:
two being the Ballance of my
Account to this Day I say £73:1:2
Wittness
Jo. Booth
Ellen EG Gwyn
her marke

14. **Nell Gwyn—a receipt to Mr. Child**—Sir Francis Child's bank in Fleet Street—only a little distance from the Palaces of Whitehall and St. James's—dealt with the affairs of many at Court. Actress Nell Gwyn, mistress of Charles II, was lent £4,600 in 1685. This receipt for the balance on her account bears her mark.

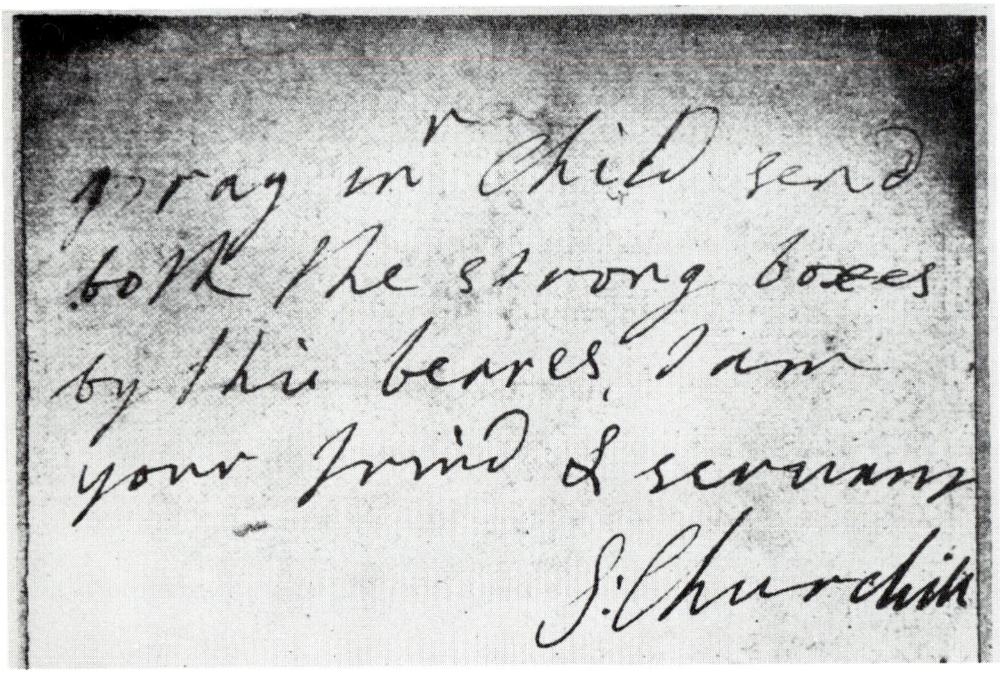
pray mr Child send
back the strong boxes
by this bearer, I am
your friend & servant
S. Churchill

15. **Sarah Churchill, Duchess of Marlborough**—This note written when she was still Lady Churchill shows Mr. Child was as willing as his latter day counterparts to hold the valuables of his customers in safe keeping.

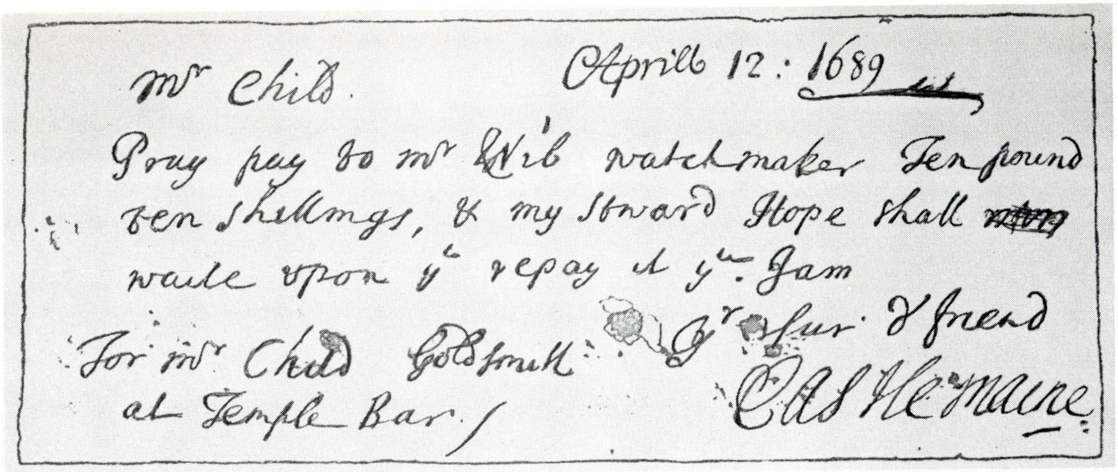
Mr Child. Aprill 12: 1689

Pray pay to mr Knib watchmaker Ten pound ten shillings, & my Steward Stope shall waile upon you & repay it you. I am

Yr Lovi: & friend

For mr Child Goldsmith at Temple Bar /

Castlemaine

16. **A "Drawn Note" by Roger, Earl of Castlemaine—on Mr. Child** — This early cheque requests Mr. Child, Goldsmith, to pay to Mr. Knibb, Clock-maker, £10.10.0. Often these drawn notes were phrased as a short letter and—as here—signed "Your Loving Friend" or with some other greeting. When Roger Castlemaine — the husband of Barbara Villiers, a rival of Nell Gwyn for the affections of Charles II—instructed his goldsmith banker to pay Knibb ten guineas he settled a bill for services or goods supplied. Joseph Knibb—one of the great names in English clockmaking whose surviving work changes hands for many thousands of pounds in the salerooms today—might have charged this amount for a silver watch. Such a figure measured in terms of purchasing power in the early 1970's might represent £200. Child's Bank was to become part of Williams & Glyn's.

17. **The Parlour at the Grasshopper**—In early banking "The Parlour" was the room in which the partners saw their clients. There has been a bank on the "Grasshopper" site in Lombard Street since the seventeenth century and on rebuilding in 1930 this gracious room was included, still known as The Parlour, and retaining the atmosphere of Georgian times.

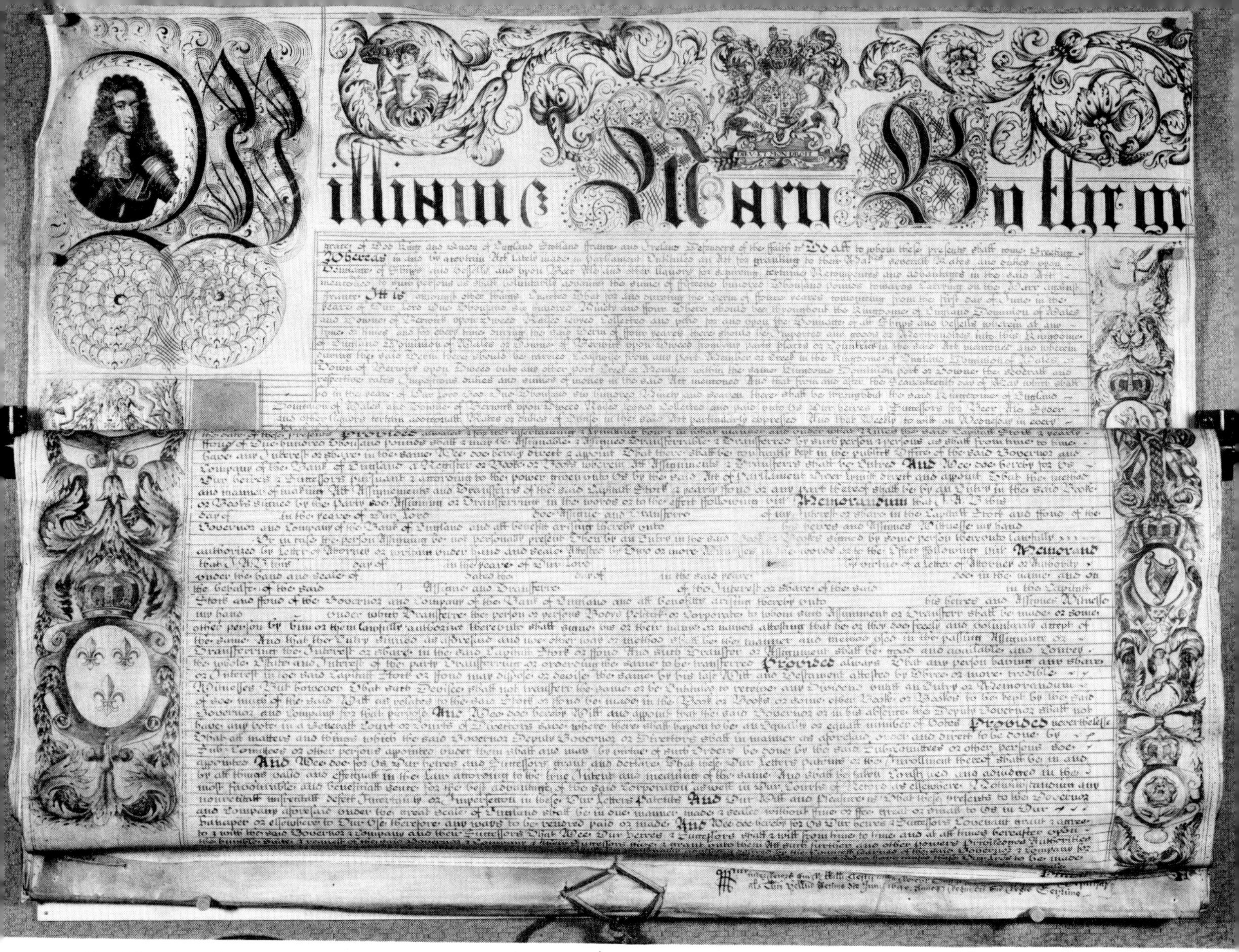

18. **The first Charter of the Bank of England**—1694 found the country at war and a government in desperate need of funds. Close relations existed with Holland, an ally whose economic development was admired and who owed much to her public banks and particularly the Bank of Amsterdam. There was constant discussion and a whole variety of plans for a national bank were canvassed. By tradition a Scot, William Paterson, is credited with the final Bank of England scheme but he may have been the mouthpiece for a powerful group of City merchants who included Sir John Houblon, later to become the Bank's first Governor. Once it was decided to form the Bank an Act was passed through Parliament, the Bank received its Charter and in twelve days raised its capital of £1,200,000. This sum was immediately lent to the government at 8 per cent.

19. **Sir John Houblon**—First Governor of the Bank of England in the critical years 1694-97. The Bank owed much to the wisdom and honesty of the early Directors. In a corrupt age, their guidance put what was little more than a large and corporate competitor of the goldsmith bankers on its long course of growth and responsibility.

20. **The Silver Tankard of 1697**—Made by the silversmith William Gamble of Foster Lane it was inscribed: "The gift of the Directors of the Bank of England to Sir John Houblon, Governor, Lord Mayor of London in token of his great ability, industry and strict uprightness at a time of extreme difficulty 1696." The tankard was lost sight of until 1893 when it re-appeared at a sale in the United States. It was acquired by the New York Clearing House Association who presented it to the Bank in 1924 as a gesture of international goodwill.

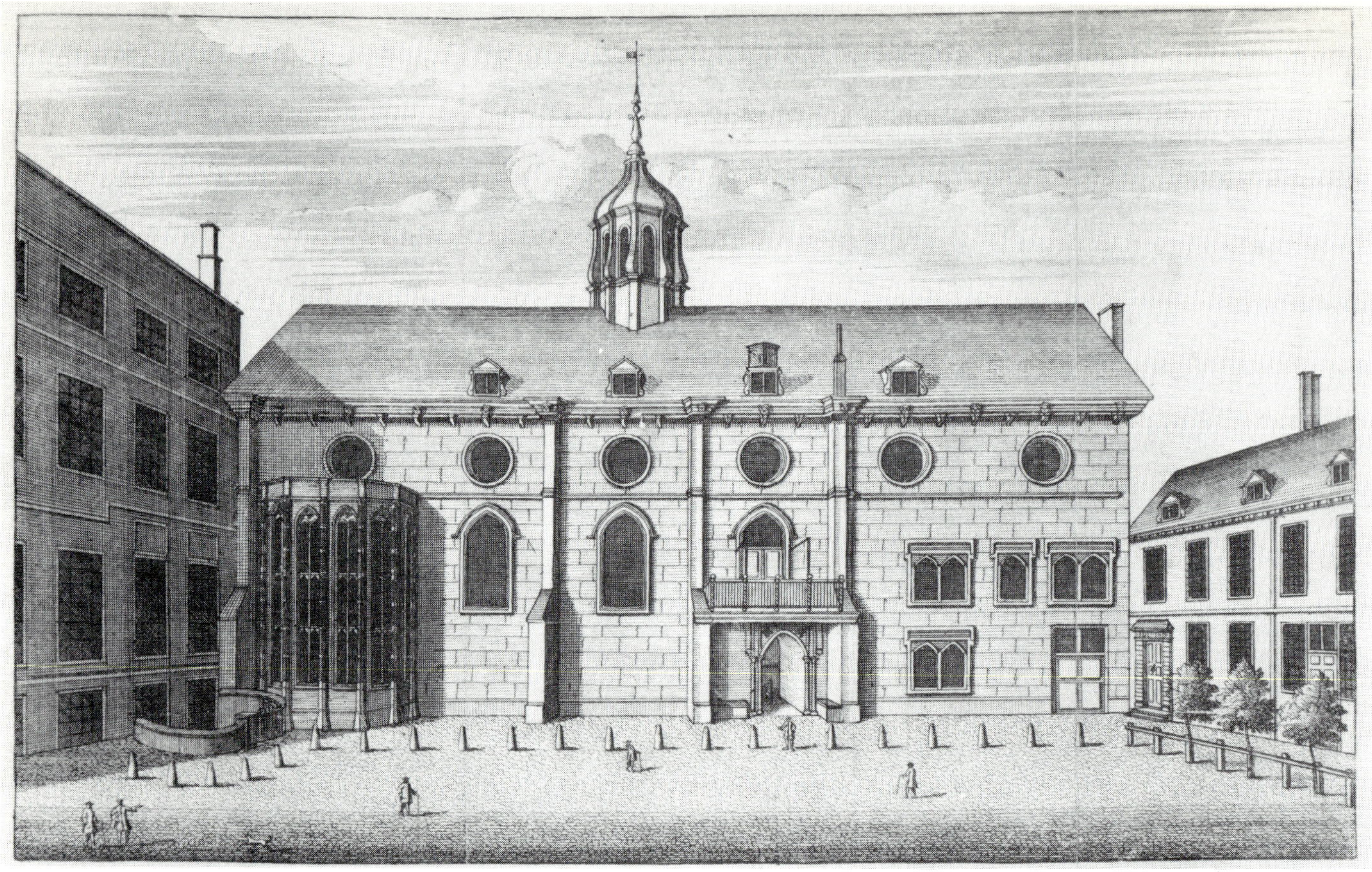

21. **The Grocers' Hall**—Original subscriptions to the Bank of England had been taken at Mercers' Hall, Cheapside, but the Bank soon transferred its business to the Grocers' Hall in the Poultry where it remained from 1695 to 1734.

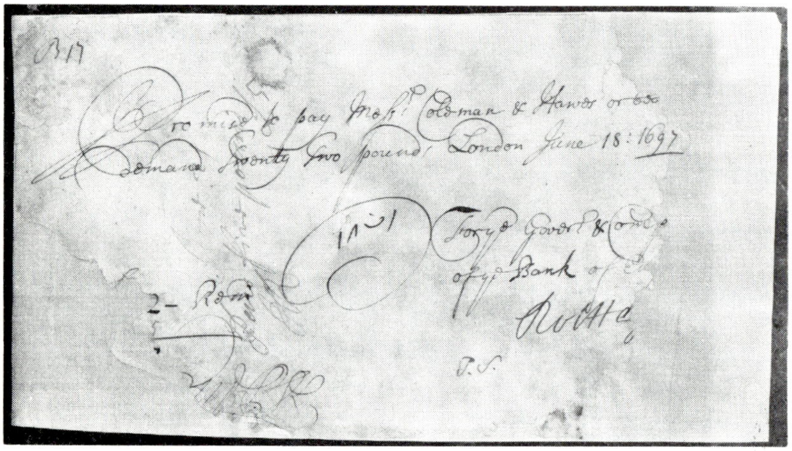

B17

Promised to pay Mess[rs] Coldman & Hawes or on demand Twenty two pounds London June 18: 1697

For ye Govr & Compa of ye Bank of

22. **The oldest Bank of England Note**—Bank notes dating from before 1700 are a great rarity. Although incomplete, this note, issued only three years after the foundation of the bank and written by hand, has the distinction of being the oldest surviving Bank of England note. It is reproduced here one quarter of the original size.

23. **An early Bank of England Note**—No. 104 for £150.8.8 dated 24 January 1699, signed by John Wase. The first notes issued by the Bank of England were not for fixed denominations but payable to a named person (or bearer) as a receipt for the amount deposited. Like any bank note they passed from hand to hand and could, if required, be cashed in part, with the note altered to show the part payment and the new amount as in this case. Shown here one quarter of its original size.

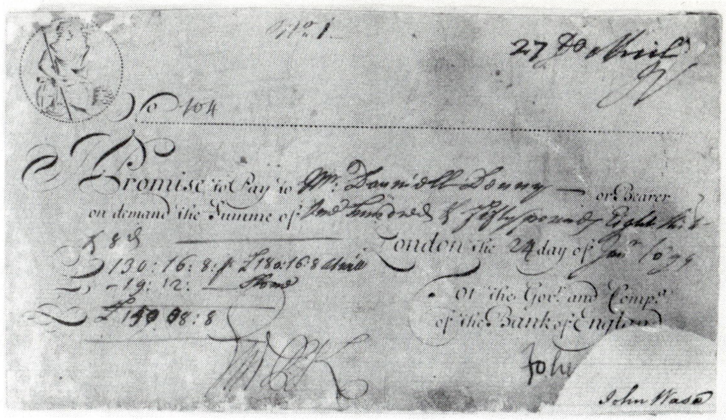

24. **A room in the Bank**—From a drawing of about 1695 showing a clerk at a desk and two merchants depositing money.

25. **Parliament Close, Edinburgh**—The Bank of Scotland. In the early part of 1695, a year after the formation of the Bank of England, a number of Scots living in London conceived the idea of a national bank in Scotland, not to support the government but to assist trade and industry. The project went well, and a constitution was drawn up, some parts being drawn from that of the Bank of England and an Act of the Scots Parliament was obtained on 17 July 1695. The Bank opened its business in Mylin Square but moved to Parliament Close in the following year.

Early Banking in Scotland—There had been Jewish money lenders and Italian "banker merchants" in Scotland since the twelfth century. Adam Tore arranged the ransom terms of King David II with the King of England and 100,000 merks were paid over in 1357. Timothy Cagniole, an Italian, appears to have stood in much the same relationship to the crown of Scotland in the sixteenth century as Gresham to the Tudors. The right to charge interest was legalised in 1687, some years later than in England. As the seventeenth century progressed there is evidence of merchants in Edinburgh who would accept deposits and remit funds in much the manner of the London goldsmiths.

▶

27. **Bank of Scotland Note**—The Bank issued notes from its formation, initially with values in sterling, of £100, £50, £20, £10 and £5. In 1704 the first notes of £1 sterling were issued. They were expressed as £12 Scots for many years despite the fact that Scots money was officially abolished in 1707.

26. **Bank of Scotland Register**—Subscriptions were taken simultaneously in Edinburgh and London on 8 November 1695. The subscription book at Edinburgh was set on a table in the tavern hall of the "Cross Keys" in Covenant Close from 1 November to 31 December 1695, when the Collector appointed collected the money offered from the 136 persons who had signed their names. The amounts are shown in pounds Scots, twelve of which were reckoned equivalent to one pound sterling. The Bank Act provided that its shareholders should be deemed naturalized Scots. In 1818 49 foreigners (French, Dutch, Italian and German) bought bank stock to qualify as British subjects. The Courts decided that foreigners could not be naturalized in this way but the clause remained in the Bank's Acts until 1920.

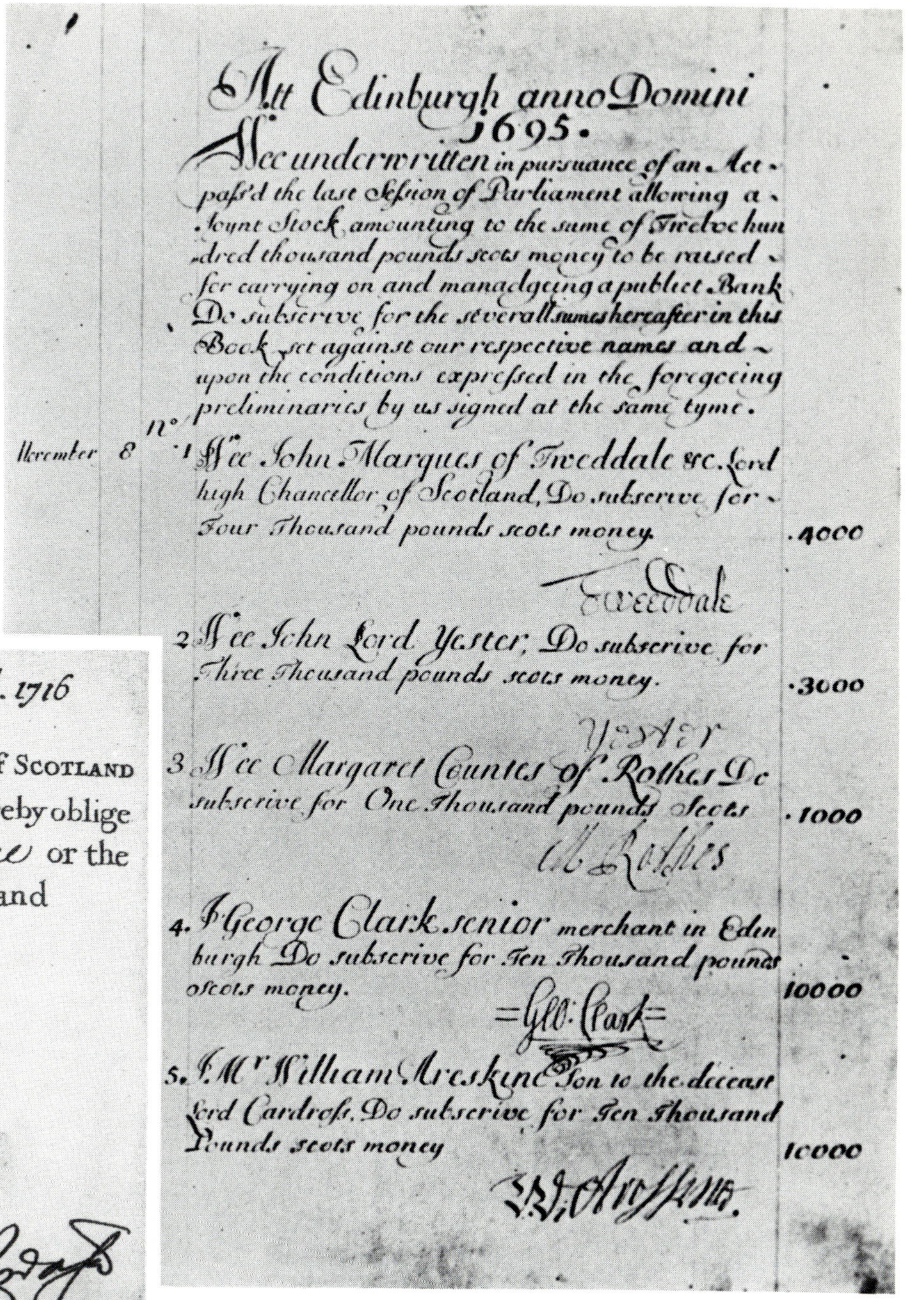
Att Edinburgh anno Domini 1695.

Wee underwritten in pursuance of an Act passd the last Session of Parliament allowing a Joynt Stock amounting to the sume of Twelve hundred thousand pounds scots money to be raised for carrying on and managing a publict Bank Do subscrive for the severall sumes hereafter in this Book set against our respective names and upon the conditions expressed in the foregoeing preliminaries by us signed at the same tyme.

November 8 No 1 Wee John Marques of Tweddale &c Lord high Chancellor of Scotland, Do subscrive for Four Thousand pounds scots money. 4000

Tweeddale

2 Wee John Lord Yester; Do subscrive for Three Thousand pounds scots money. 3000

Yester

3 Wee Margaret Countes of Rothes Do subscrive for One Thousand pounds Scots 1000

M Rothes

4. I George Clark senior merchant in Edinburgh Do subscrive for Ten Thousand pounds scots money. 10000

Geo: Clark

5. I Mr William Areskine Son to the deceast Lord Cardross Do subscrive for Ten Thousand Pounds scots money 10000

W Areskine

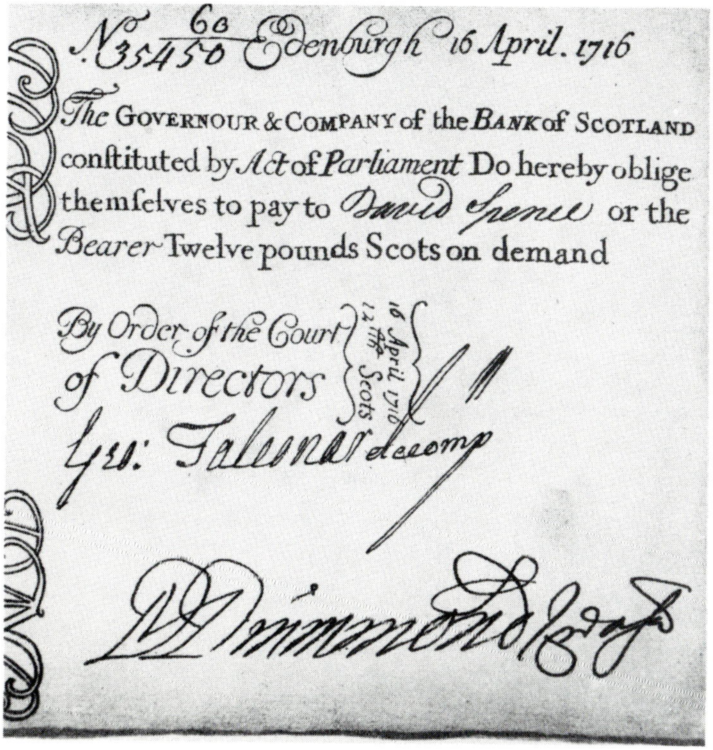
No 60/35450 Edenburgh 16 April. 1716

The GOVERNOUR & COMPANY of the BANK of SCOTLAND constituted by Act of Parliament Do hereby oblige themselves to pay to David Spence or the Bearer Twelve pounds Scots on demand

By Order of the Court of Directors

16 April 1716 12 lib Scots

Geo: Falconar Accomp

Drummond

28. **The "Virginia Don"**—Although the Bank of Scotland opened four branches these were closed down for various reasons before the close of the seventeenth century. The Royal Bank of Scotland did not open until 1727 and the British Linen Company until 1746. A single bank could not serve a whole country from Edinburgh and in the first part of the eighteenth century and later, influential and wealthy merchants lent money, discounted bills and accepted large deposits. Such was the "Virginia Don", a "Tobacco Lord" of the 1730's, here shown accepting a deposit from some Highland trader.

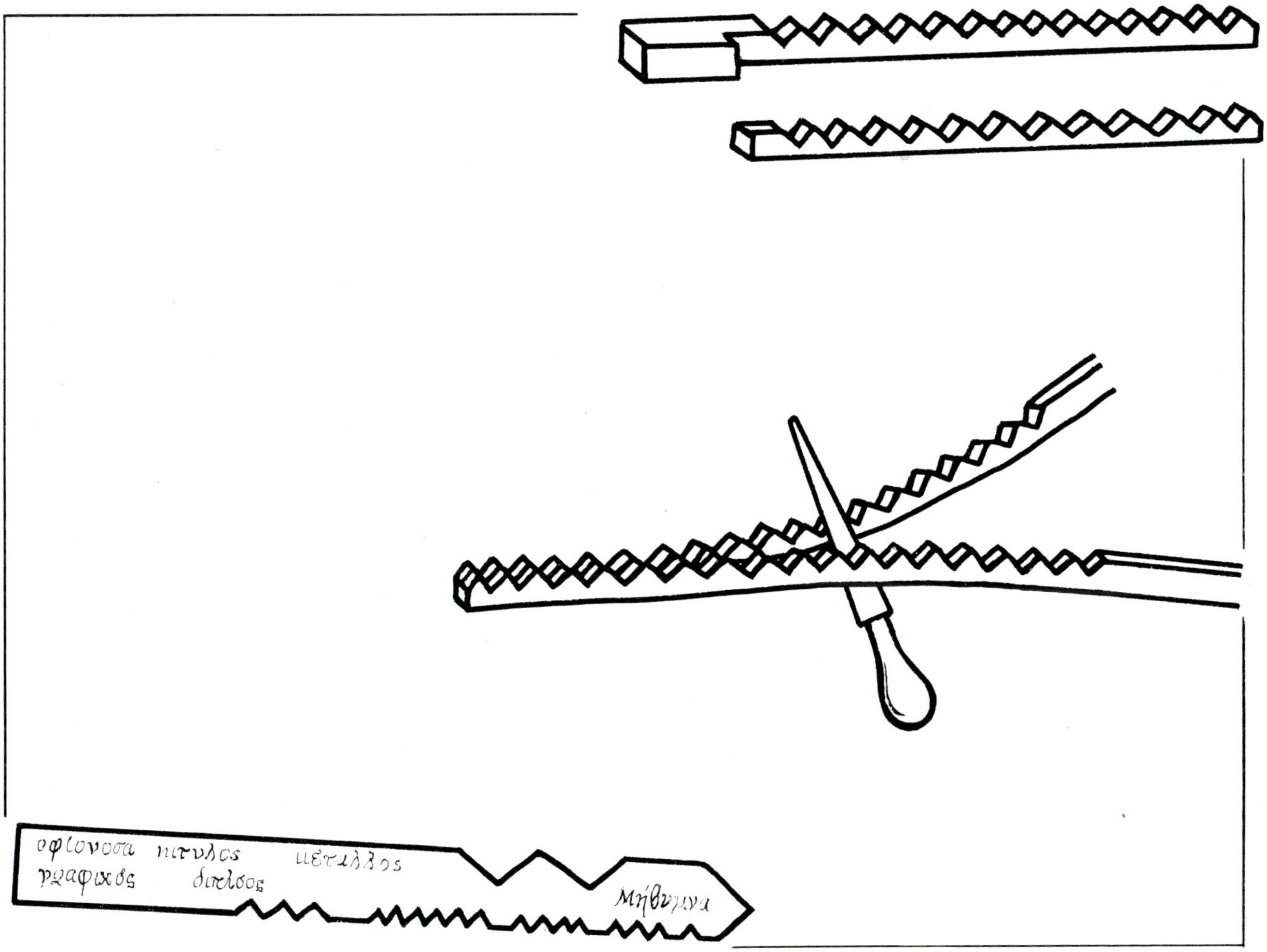

29. **Tallies**—These were willow sticks up to eight feet long and one inch broad notched to indicate sums loaned to the Government. The stick was then split down the middle with one half handed to the lender and the other retained by the Exchequer. On repayment the two halves were matched together. The Bank of England's only receipt for the advances of £1,200,000 made to the government from its original capital were tallies such as these. Tallies were abolished in 1826 and it is interesting to note that the burning of old tally sticks caused the fire which destroyed the Houses of Parliament in 1834.

In the illustration the large notches on the top of the stick record hundreds and on the bottom show tens and units of pounds, shillings, pence and halfpence. On the stick was written in Latin the name of the borrower, the rate of interest and the Government Fund from which interest would be paid. The amount shown by the notches in this illustration is £236. 4s. 3½d (See also 112).

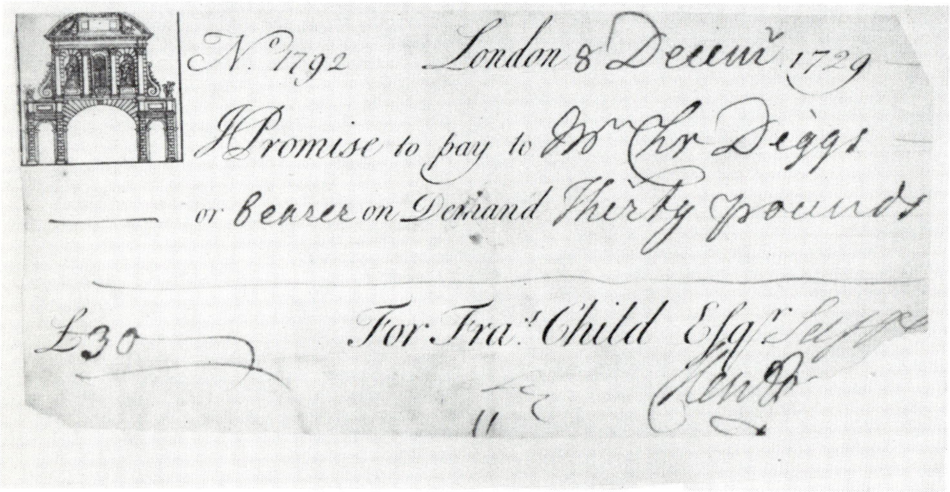

No. 1792 London 8 Decem.r 1729

I Promise to pay to Mr Chr Diggs or bearer on Demand Thirty pounds

£30

For Fra.s Child Esq.r

31. **Early printed bank note of Sir Francis Child**—Early notes were hand written but the Bank of England soon adopted partly printed bank notes of a kind it used for well over a hundred years. Francis Child, the Fleet Street banker, used printed notes from 1729 onwards and this earliest surviving example was issued in that year.

30. **Fleet Street, showing Temple Bar**—Dated 1753, Maurer's print shows a bustling thoroughfare leading from the City to the West End. Hoare's Golden Bottle sign must hang in the shadows on the extreme left at what became No. 37. Child's Bank lies just this side of a Temple Bar which still carries on iron spikes the grim crop of the heads of executed traitors. Child's became No. 1, and midway between is the bank of Goslings at the sign of "Ye Three Squirrels"—later to be No. 19.

32. **Sir Francis Child's jewel ledger**—As with all goldsmith bankers, Child carried on his goldsmith business side by side with his banking activities. He lent jewels to Queen Mary for her coronation at a rent of £222. He is believed to have concentrated on banking soon after 1700 but this ledger in his own handwriting—describing and pricing rings, with a diagram showing every stone—indicates that the change had not yet been fully made.

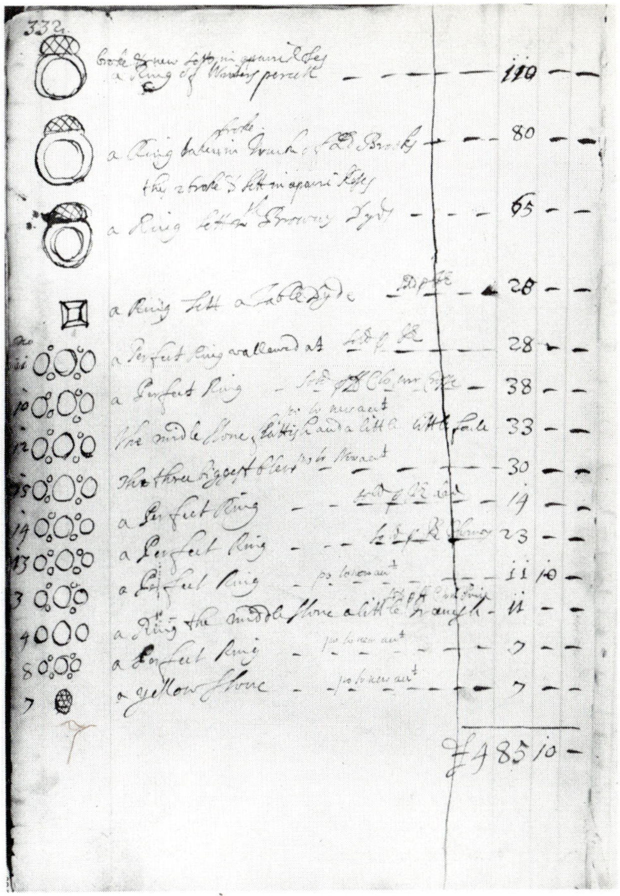

332

a Ring ... 110

a Ring ... 80

a Ring ... 65

a Ring ... 20

a Perfect Ring ... 28

a Perfect Ring ... 38

the middle stone ... 33

the three biggest stones ... 30

a Perfect Ring ... 19

a Perfect Ring ... 23

a Perfect Ring ... 11 10

a Ring the middle stone ... 11

a Perfect Ring ... 7

a yellow stone ... 7

£485 10

33. **Goslings Ledger account of Thomas Pitt**—In 1719 the Fleet Street bank, later to become Goslings and Sharpe, was a partnership of George Wanley and George Cradock. It had the account of Thomas Pitt, an Anglo-Indian "nabob". The father of William Pitt, Lord Chatham and grandfather of William Pitt the Younger, he was Governor of Madras. He bought the famous Pitt diamond in the rough for £2,400 and sold the polished stone to the Crown of France for £200,000 (perhaps £50,000 and £4,000,000 by present values). At this period no pass book or statement was issued and a customer periodically inspected the bank's ledger and if satisfied signed it as agreeing the balance.

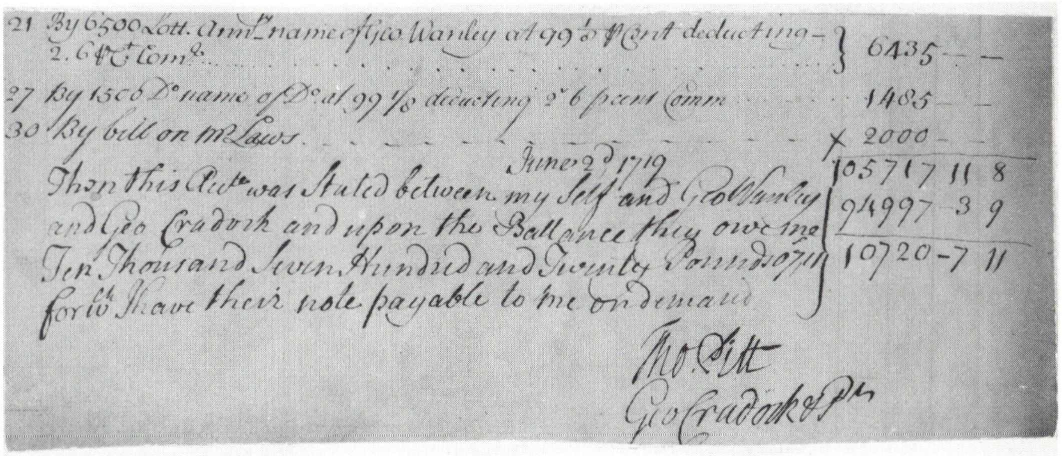

21 By 6500 Lott. Amt. name of Geo. Wanley at 99½ P Cent deducting 2.6 P Ct Comn. } 6435

27 By 1500 Do name of Do at 99½ deducting 2s 6 p cent Comm 1485

30 By bill on Mr Laws 2000

105717 11 8

94997 3 9

June 2d 1719

Then this Acct was Stated between my Self and Geo Wanley and Geo Cradock and upon the Ballance they owe me Ten Thousand Seven Hundred and Twenty Pounds 07 11 for wch I have their note payable to me on demand } 10720 7 11

Tho. Pitt

Geo Cradock & Pt

40. **Country Banking, Abel Collin's Ledger** — Although a banking system was well established in London by the 1660's difficult travel over appalling roads gave no encouragement to the goldsmith bankers to establish branches in the provinces. Industry was expanding in the North and Midlands and banks were eventually established by the local brewer, ironmaster, attorney or shopkeeper. Providing they had the trust of their fellow townsmen, they could take deposits and issue bank notes without restriction of any kind. How far the provinces lagged behind is shown by a statement in the middle of the eighteenth century that there were only a dozen bankers' shops outside London. Not all can be identified but the oldest was almost certainly Smiths' of Nottingham. In 1704 Abel Collin, a Nottingham mercer, died and left the residue of his estate to build a hospital. A bank account would have been opened in 1709, the ledger is open at the page for 1748 and the account is in operation to this day at Smiths' Bank branch of the National Westminster Bank at Nottingham. Note the price of 36 tons of coal, £11.5.0d.

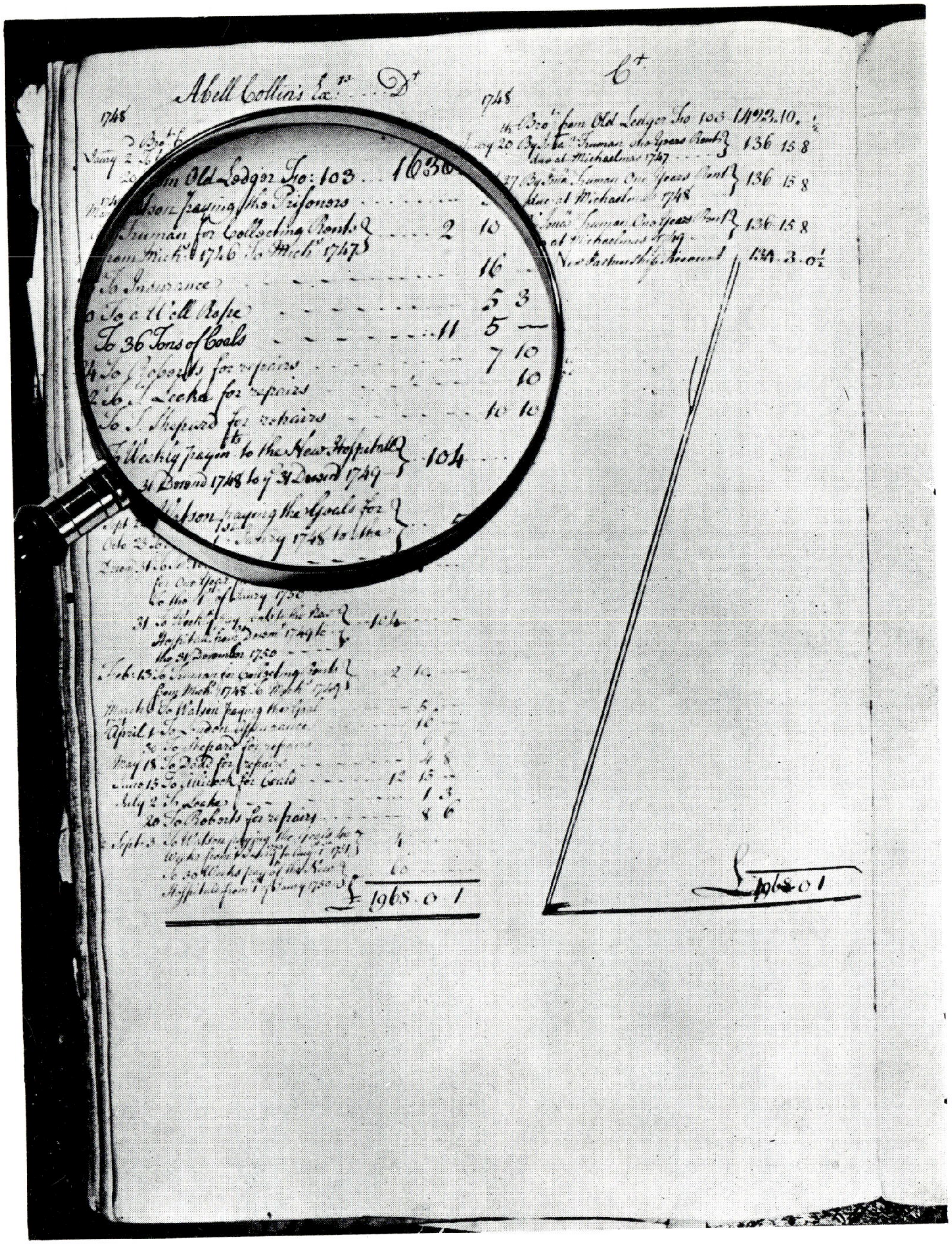

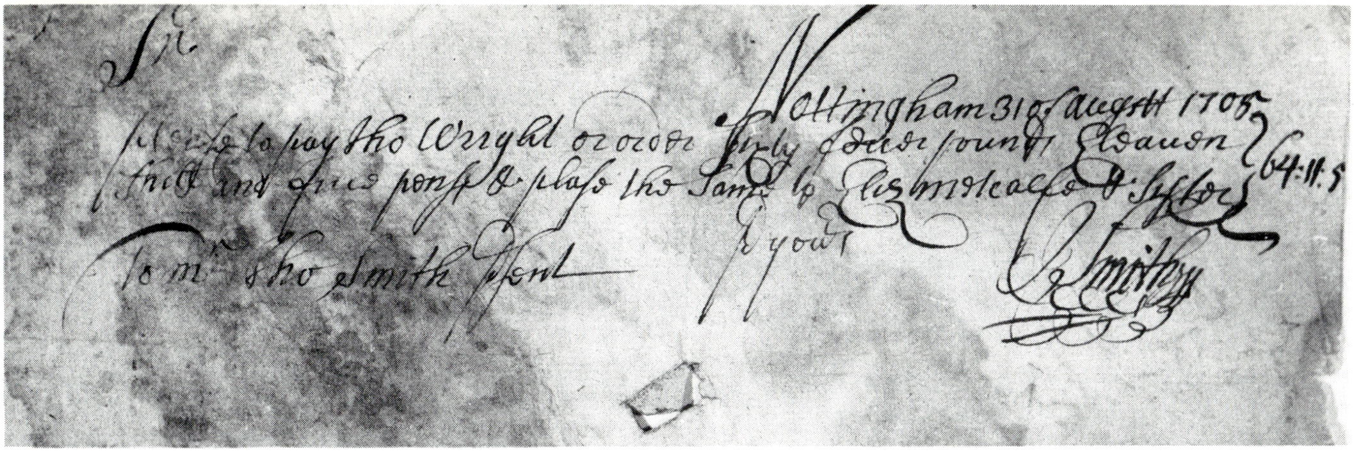
Sir

Nottingham 31 of august 1705

pleas to pay Tho Wright or order Sixty foure pounds Eleaven

shill and fiue pence & plase the Same to Eliz metcalfe & Sister

£64:11:5

yours

Smith

To Mr Tho Smith present

41. **Smiths' Bank, Nottingham, 1705**—The earliest surviving cheque on a country banker, for £64.11.5d., was drawn on Smiths' in 1705.

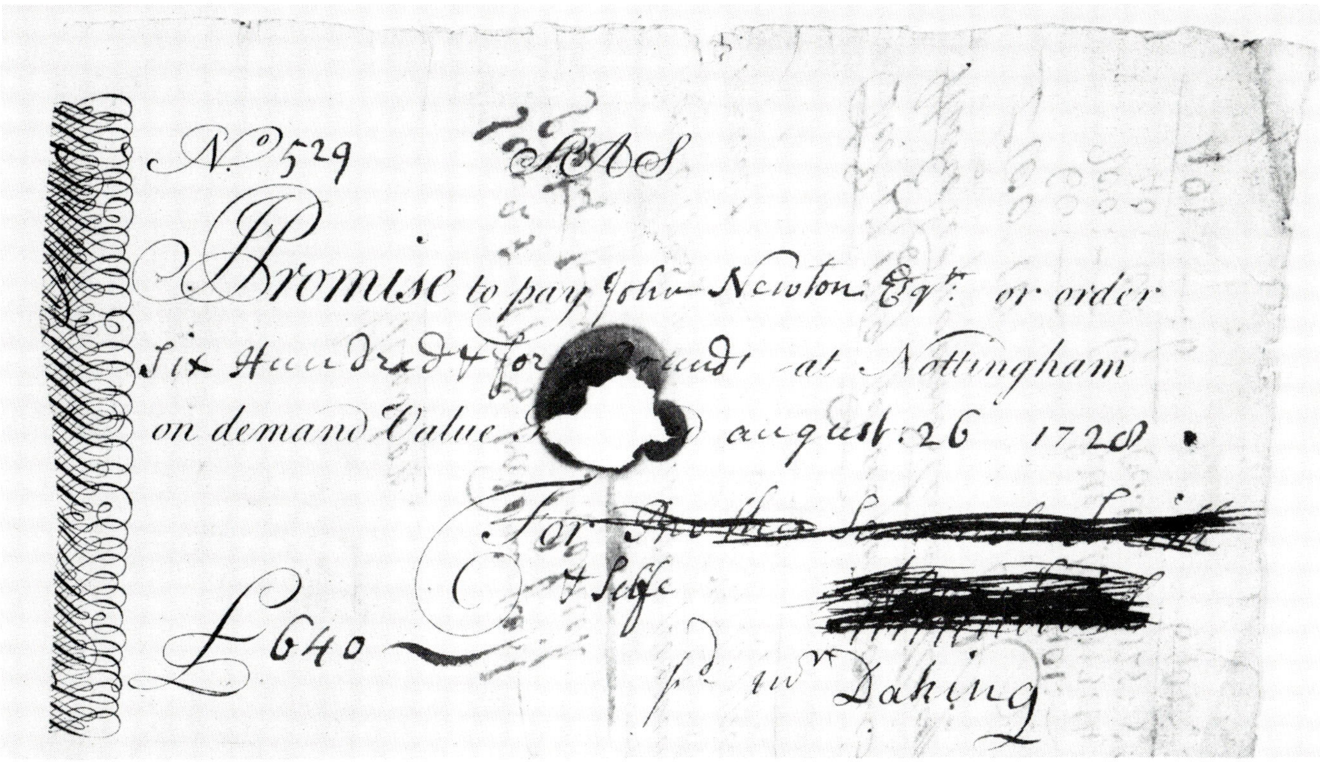
No 529

I Promise to pay John Newton Esqr. or order

Six Hundred & for[illegible] Pounds at Nottingham

on demand Value [illegible] august: 26 1728.

For [illegible]

& Selfe

£640

pd Mr Daking

42. **Smiths' Bank, Nottingham, 1728**—The earliest surviving bank note issued by a provincial banker is one for £640 issued on 26 August 1728 by Smiths' Bank.

43. **The Great Iron Chest in the Parlours**—Strong boxes were used to protect valuables whether in a private home or a merchant's shop. The Bank of England used such boxes in its early years and this one is still in its possession. Another is shown in the previous drawing (24).

44. **Sampson Lloyd**—Prompted by Abel Smith, the Nottingham banker, Sampson Lloyd II joined John Taylor to found the first formal banking business in Birmingham on 3 June 1765. Lloyd, a Quaker ironmaster, had been involved in the tremendous growth of the Birmingham iron trade in the first half of the eighteenth century. Taylor, originally a cabinet maker, a friend of Dr. Johnson, and known as "our great button maker", was a man of wealth. The fusion of business experience, local knowledge and wealth on which many of the successful country bankers were founded is well illustrated by this partnership. In the title "Taylors and Lloyds" the name of the younger man came first, probably because he was wealthier and better known in Birmingham. However, Sampson Lloyd II was the inspiration of the bank, and time has seen justice done in the title of the great modern bank which bears his name.

45. **Taylors and Lloyds, Birmingham Bank, Seven Shilling Note**—An act of 1775 prohibited the issue of bank notes of less than £1. This note for a third of a guinea was issued just before that date and the firm also issued notes for a quarter of a guinea. It was required that three—or four—had to be presented together for payment of a guinea.

46. **Birmingham Old Bank**—Taylors and Lloyds had their first premises at Dale End in Birmingham and moved to this building in High Street which became the Head Office of the Bank from 1815 to 1871. The building had formerly been the house of John Taylor, one of the original partners.

47. **Backhouse & Co., Five Guinea Note**—Originally linen and worsted manufacturers in Darlington, the Backhouse family were already engaged in banking business, to assist tradesmen and farmers, when they formally opened their bank in 1774. Their notes were payable at Darlington, and at their London agents. They were one of a number of Quaker families in eighteenth and nineteenth century banking, successful men of business with a reputation for honesty and fair dealing. As Quakers they refused to use months named after Roman Gods and this note is dated for the 8th of the 11th month 1779 rather than for November.

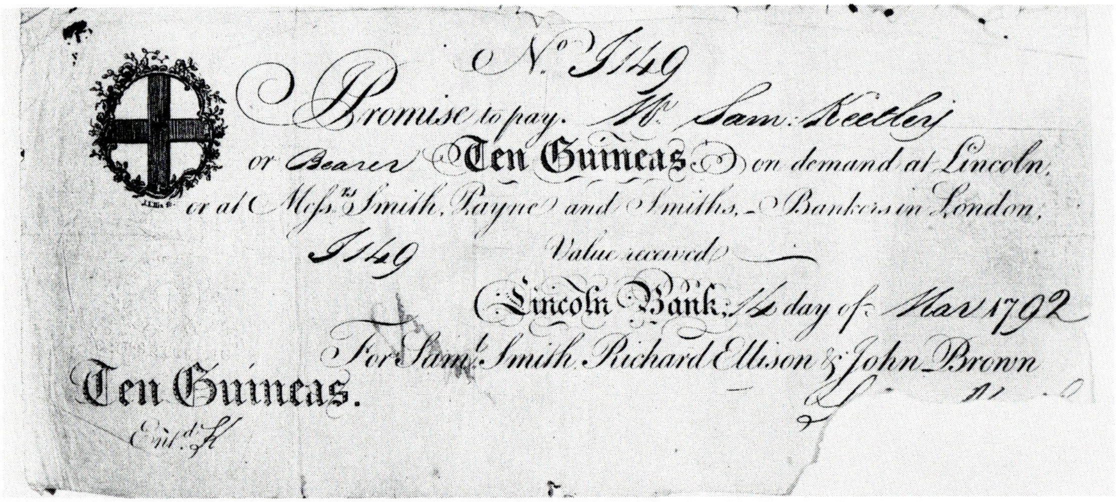

48. **Lincoln Bank, Ten Guinea Note**—Abel Smith II the Nottingham banker founded a bank in London in 1758, one in Hull in 1784 and the Lincoln Bank in 1775. The Lincoln partnership issued notes of varying amounts such as £5, 5 guineas, £10, 10 guineas, £20, £25, £50. A note for £500 was issued in 1775. A 9 guinea note—which saved the higher stamp duty of a 10 guinea one—was used in the 1780's. As the golden guinea was the standard coin, notes in guineas were more useful than those in pounds. The life of these notes was short and they came back to the Bank for payment on average three to four months after issue.

49. **Royal Bank of Scotland "option" bank note**—The Royal Bank of Scotland was founded in 1727. After early and bitter struggles with the Bank of Scotland, it had become well established by 1762 when this "option" note was issued. Valued at £1 sterling—and still marked £12 Scots—it was payable on demand or, at the option of the Bank, six months after the date of demand with interest of six pence. A convenient way of checking a "run" on a bank, "option" clauses were abolished by an Act of 1765.

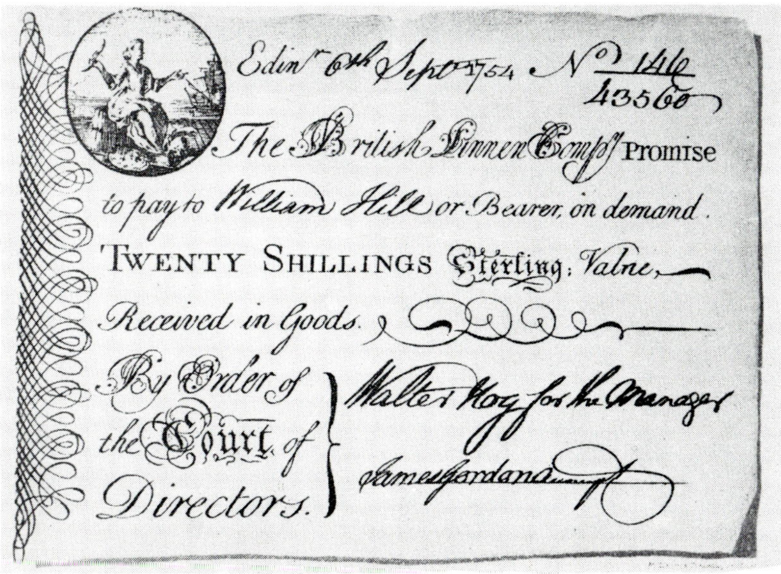

50. **British Linen Co. Promissory Note 1754**—The third of the "big three" in early Scottish banking was founded by Royal Charter in 1746 "to carry on the Linen Manufactory in all its Branches". In the 1760's the Company moved into banking, at first to the linen trade and later in the decade to other commercial customers. All interest in linen appears to have ceased by the end of the eighteenth century but it was not until 1906 that the title was changed to British Linen Bank. The Mark of the bank's origins remained until quite recently when it merged with the Bank of Scotland. This promissory note, issued in payment for linen goods, dates from the pre-banking era.

51. **The London Clearing House**—By 1770 the cheque system had developed in London and banks daily received from customers cheques, drawn on other banks, to be credited to their accounts. The clerks who were sent to obtain cash for these cheques soon found it easier to meet at one central point where an exchange could take place and with only the difference in totals between banks settled in cash. They met at a chop house called the "Five Bells", in Dove Court off Lombard Street. Presently the banks realised the advantage of the scheme and rented a quieter meeting place nearby. Thus they put on an official basis the Clearing House, which still stands near the site of the "Five Bells".

52. **Recoinage 1774**—It was not until the nineteenth century that this country had an ample supply of sound coin in daily use. Earlier no provision was made for the periodic renewal of gold, silver or copper coins and those in circulation became worn. Before the use of a milled edge, coins were "clipped" by cutting away small parts at the edge. The good work of a recoinage in 1696 had long since passed when in 1760 it was recorded that all crowns and most half crowns had vanished from circulation and the average shilling was reduced to five-sixths and the sixpence to three quarters of its nominal weight. Gold was also badly worn and in 1774 all light guineas were withdrawn in exchange for "new and perfect coin". The exchange took place through agents appointed by the government—one of whom was the Exeter Bank—a parallel of the part taken by the banks in the decimalization of February 1971. The cost to the Treasury was over £500,000 but it was money well spent. Nothing, however, was done about silver and copper—a problem for many years to come.

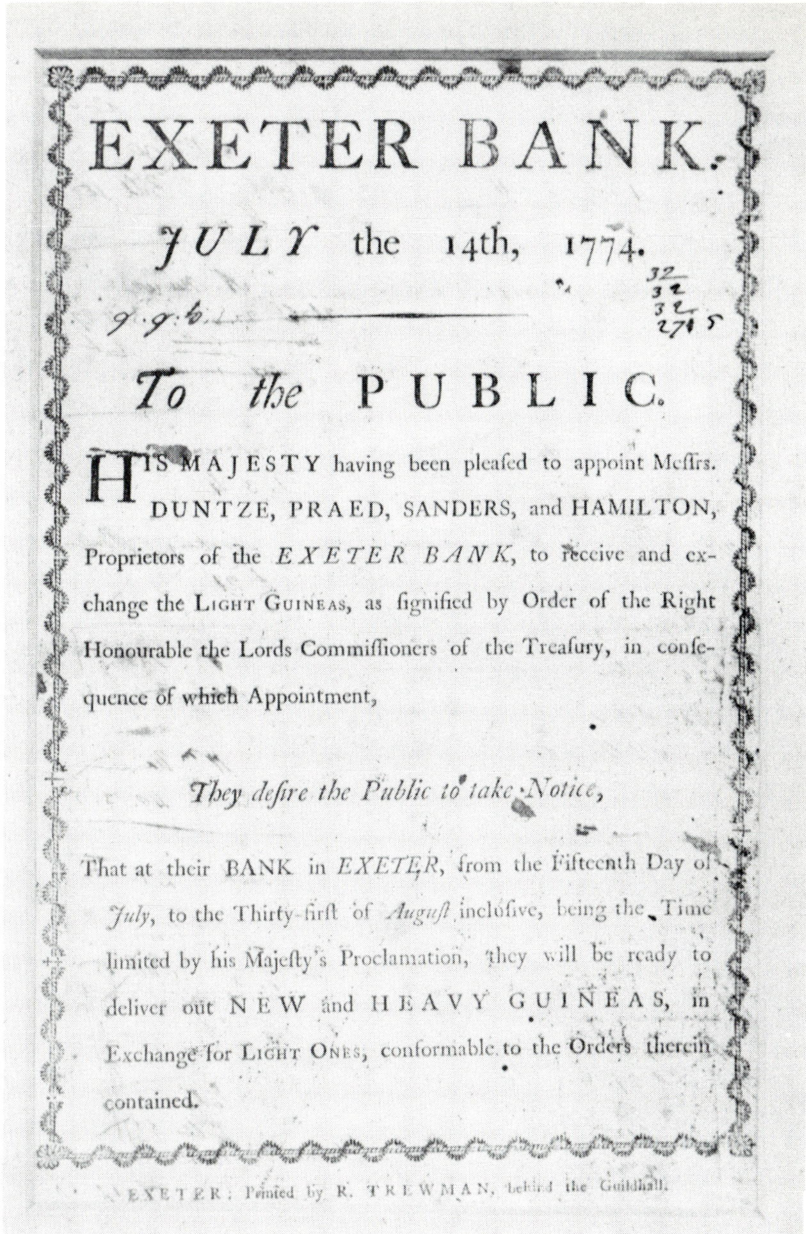

EXETER BANK.

JULY the 14th, 1774.

To the PUBLIC.

HIS MAJESTY having been pleaſed to appoint Meſſrs. DUNTZE, PRAED, SANDERS, and HAMILTON, Proprietors of the *EXETER BANK*, to receive and exchange the LIGHT GUINEAS, as ſignified by Order of the Right Honourable the Lords Commiſſioners of the Treaſury, in conſequence of which Appointment,

They deſire the Public to take Notice,

That at their BANK in *EXETER*, from the Fifteenth Day of *July*, to the Thirty-firſt of *Auguſt* incluſive, being the Time limited by his Majeſty's Proclamation, they will be ready to deliver out NEW and HEAVY GUINEAS, in Exchange for LIGHT ONES, conformable to the Orders therein contained.

EXETER: Printed by R. TREWMAN, behind the Guildhall.

53. **Abraham Newland**—The Bank of England appears to have been loyally served by its employees in the eighteenth century. It is said that in his thirty years as Chief Cashier (1778-1807) Newland never slept away from the Bank. Although he sometimes drove to his cottage at Highbury for tea he always returned to the Bank during the evening. Since his name appeared on the Bank notes in the space provided for the payee's name for so many years these notes were popularly known as "Abraham Newlands". It was not until 1855 that the Bank discontinued naming its Chief Cashier as payee on every note.

54. **Bank of England—Taylor's Transfer Offices**—As the Bank's business grew during the eighteenth century, Sampson's original buildings were outgrown and additions were made at various times. When the Bank Charter was renewed in 1764 the architect Sir Robert Taylor designed extensions which included these Transfer Offices.

55. **Bank of England—Taylor's Rotunda**—Between two of the Transfer Offices Taylor built the Rotunda modelled on the Pantheon in Rome. This drawing by Thomas Rowlandson shows the bustle and confusion when used as a stock exchange. Some time after the Stock Exchange had obtained buildings for itself the remaining users were described in 1806 as being "by no means of a reputable description, consisting in general of persons who will not subscribe to the Stock Exchange or have been excluded, female jobbers and idle persons". It was not until 1838 that they were finally expelled.

56. **Gordon Riots, 1780**—In June 1780 the London mob took to the streets in an orgy of pillage and looting. The excuse was religious and for two days the Irish Catholic district of Moorfield was sacked and burned. Before the days of a regular police force the Government could only bring in troops but were unable to act since no magistrate could be found who would read the Riot Act. Brackley Kennet the Lord Mayor was secretly sympathetic to the anti-Catholic cause and stood inactive until on the 6th the mob burned down Newgate Prison and moved on to take the Bank of England with its gold. The Lord Mayor applied for troops who were able to garrison both the Bank itself and the church and tower of St. Christopher-le-Stocks which at that time stood beside the Bank. The troops, with three cannon and reinforced by militia as well as civilian volunteers, repulsed a number of attacks and some of the mob were killed and many wounded. This drawing illustrates the scene at the height of the attack. The Bank opened for essential business the following day but the military remained for several weeks.

57. **The Bank of England and the Royal Exchange in 1790**—The need for expansion and the danger shown by the Gordon Riots led to the purchase and demolition of the church of St. Christopher-le-Stocks, thus removing the tower from which the Bank premises could be brought under musket fire. This picture by William Marlow shows Sampson's central gatehouse (1732) and Taylor's wings, the first to the right (1765) and the second replacing the church to the left (1782). The second Royal Exchange—still carrying Thomas Gresham's grasshoppers on its spire and masts—lies behind the triangular building.

58. **The Bank Picquet**—From the time of the Gordon Riots in June 1780 until July 1973 there was a permanent night guard at the Bank of England drawn from the Guards battalion on London duty. In its early days the arrangement was resented by the City authorities—a resentment voiced in pictorial form in James Gillray's "The March to the Bank" purporting to show the ill treatment of citizens by soldiers on their way to take up guard.

▶

60. **Liverpool Corporation "Bank" Note**—By an Act of 1793 the Corporation of Liverpool obtained the power "to issue negotiable notes for a limited time and to a limited amount of £3,000,000". Liverpool is probably the only local authority to obtain this right. The issue enabled funds to be raised on the credit of the Corporation in a period of crisis after the outbreak of war with France in 1793. All notes were withdrawn and repaid by 1796.

59. The "Grasshopper" Arms—Every bank had weapons to protect its valuables and its staff. It is said that the arms shown here were purchased at the time of the 1745 Rebellion and the "Grasshopper" partnership records of 10 January 1765 show a receipt for their cleaning. They were used at the time of the 1780 Riots and remain in the hall of 68 Lombard Street to this day. In 1940, the City Police required that the muskets should be locked in the strong room for fear that German parachutists might seize them on landing.

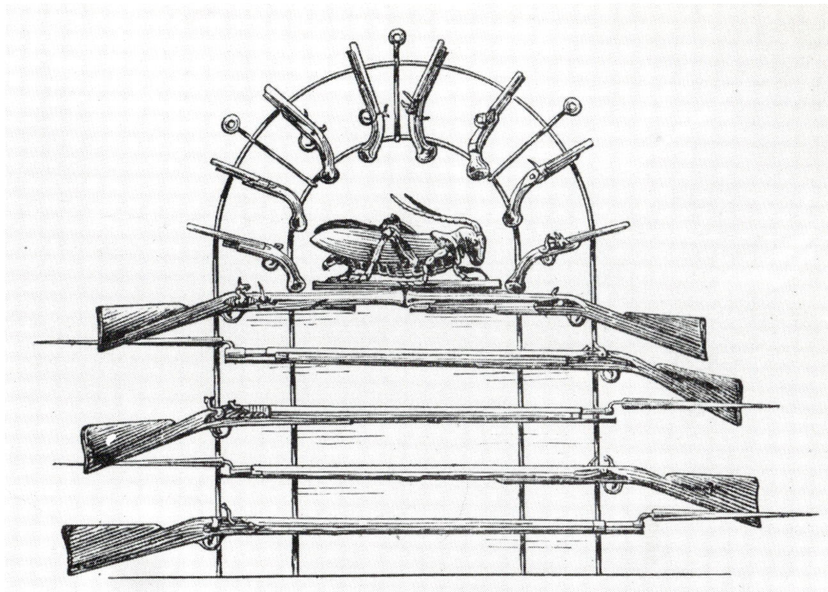

61. **Gurneys of Norwich**—This Quaker family had long been established as merchants in Norwich when in 1775 they opened their bank and, as with so many other country bankers, they are believed to have carried out banking type transactions for their fellow traders long before this date. The bank moved to this Georgian building in Redwell Plain (now Bank Plain) in 1777 and has remained on the site to this day. Gurneys were one of the most important of the private bankers, many of Quaker origin, who came together as Barclay & Co Ltd in 1896.

62. **Norwich and Norfolk Bank Note 1836**—This note issued by the Gurney Norwich partnership was payable on demand either at Norwich or at their London Agents, Barclay, Bevan, Tritton & Co.

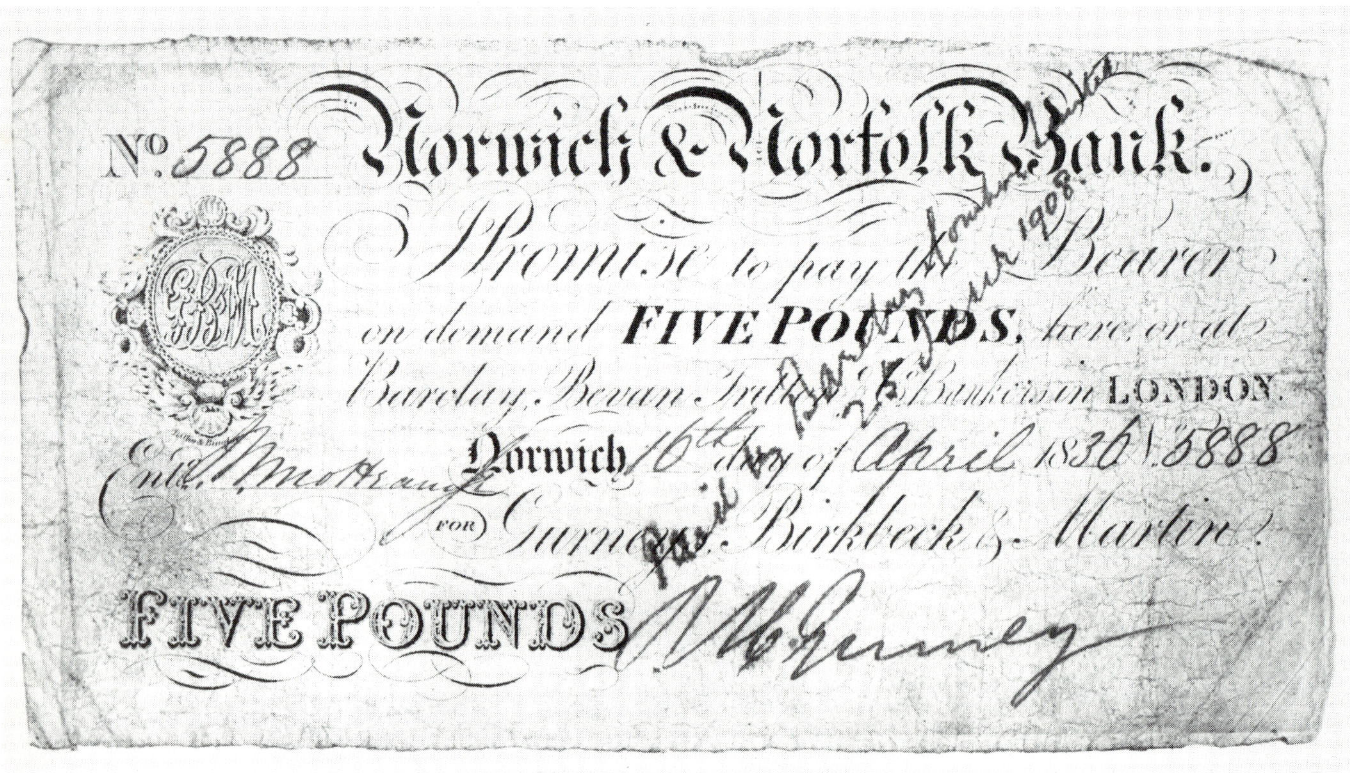

63. **St. Edmund the King and Martyr and 58 Lombard Street**—Amongst all the changes in Lombard Street over the last three centuries the church of St. Edmund the King has remained unaltered. The property to the right has given way to Barclays Bank Head Office, a bank which can claim descent from the Lombard Street goldsmith John Freame who was in business before 1694 and in 1728 moved to the premises known as "The Black Spread Eagle". This house later became No. 56 a part of the present-day Head Office site and the sign remains the house badge of Barclays.

64. **Tellson's Bank and "A Tale of Two Cities"**—By the early nineteenth century banks had become sufficiently a part of national life to find mention in Charles Dickens' novel "A Tale of Two Cities". An illustration by "Phiz" sets the scene when Mr. Styver, passing Tellson's Bank at Temple Bar, calls to see Mr. Lorry 'in his musty back closet'. "Here" says Dickens, "the clerks were kept like cheeses till they acquired the full Tellson flavour and the blue mould."

65. **Letter of Credit 1786**—The wealthy young nobleman making the "grand tour" might be away from England for several years. Already Letters of Credit, which could be drawn against as cash, were issued by London bankers available with their correspondents throughout Europe. This letter—issued by Pall Mall bankers Ransom & Co. in French, then the language of diplomacy and commerce—could be used in every town of any size in continental Europe. Such was the forerunner of the travellers cheque.

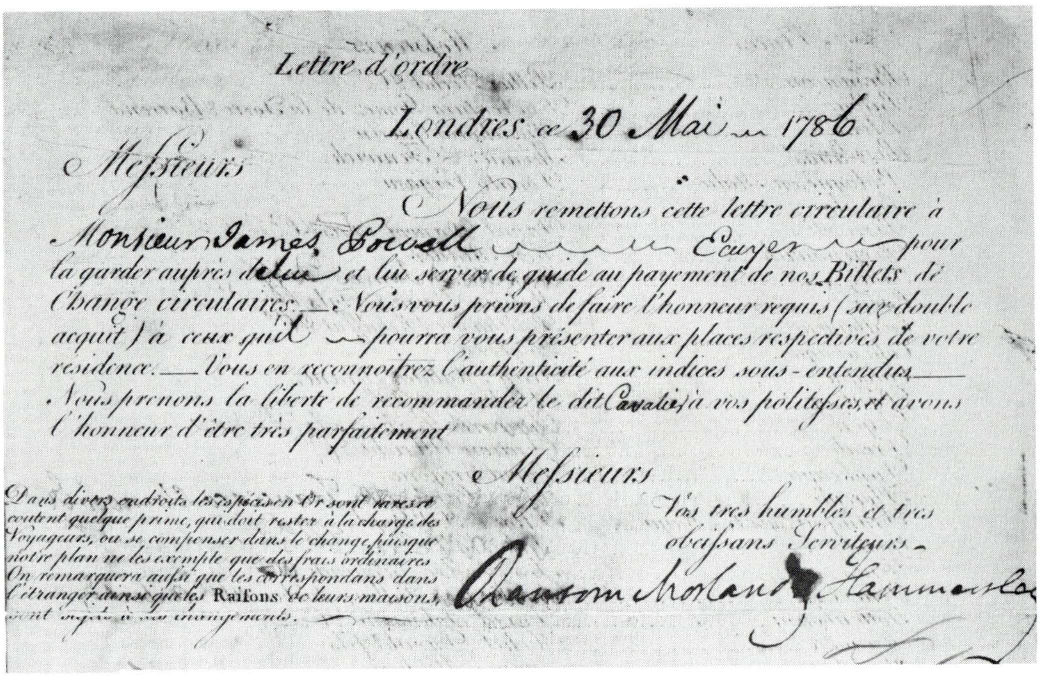

Lettre d'ordre

Londres ce 30 Mai 1786

Messieurs

Nous remettons cette lettre circulaire à Monsieur James Powell Ecuyer pour la garder auprès de lui et lui servir de guide au payement de nos Billets de Change circulaires.— Nous vous prions de faire l'honneur requis (sur double acquit) à ceux qu'il pourra vous présenter aux places respectives de votre résidence.— Vous en reconnoitrez l'authenticité aux indices sous-entendus.— Nous prenons la liberté de recommander le dit Cavalier à vos politesses, et avons l'honneur d'être très parfaitement

Messieurs

Vos très humbles et très obéissans Serviteurs

Ransom Morland & Hammersley

Dans divers endroits les espèces en Or sont [illegible] coûtent quelque prime, qui doit rester à la charge des Voyageurs, ou se compenser dans le change, puisque notre plan ne les exempte que des frais ordinaires. On remarquera aussi que les correspondans dans l'étranger ainsi que les Raisons de leurs maisons, sont sujets à des changements.

66. **"Political Ravishment" or The Old Lady of Threadneedle Street in danger**!—In 1795 and 1796 the government of William Pitt borrowed large sums to prosecute the war against France. By January 1797 the Bank of England Directors were alarmed at the way their gold reserves were draining away and asked for repayment. By February it was clear the Bank might have to close its doors and on the 26th a proclamation suspended the Bank's obligation to pay out in gold against its notes. Gillray's cartoon shows Pitt attacking the Old Lady of Threadneedle Street seated on her money chest. This is the earliest known reference to the Bank by this name.

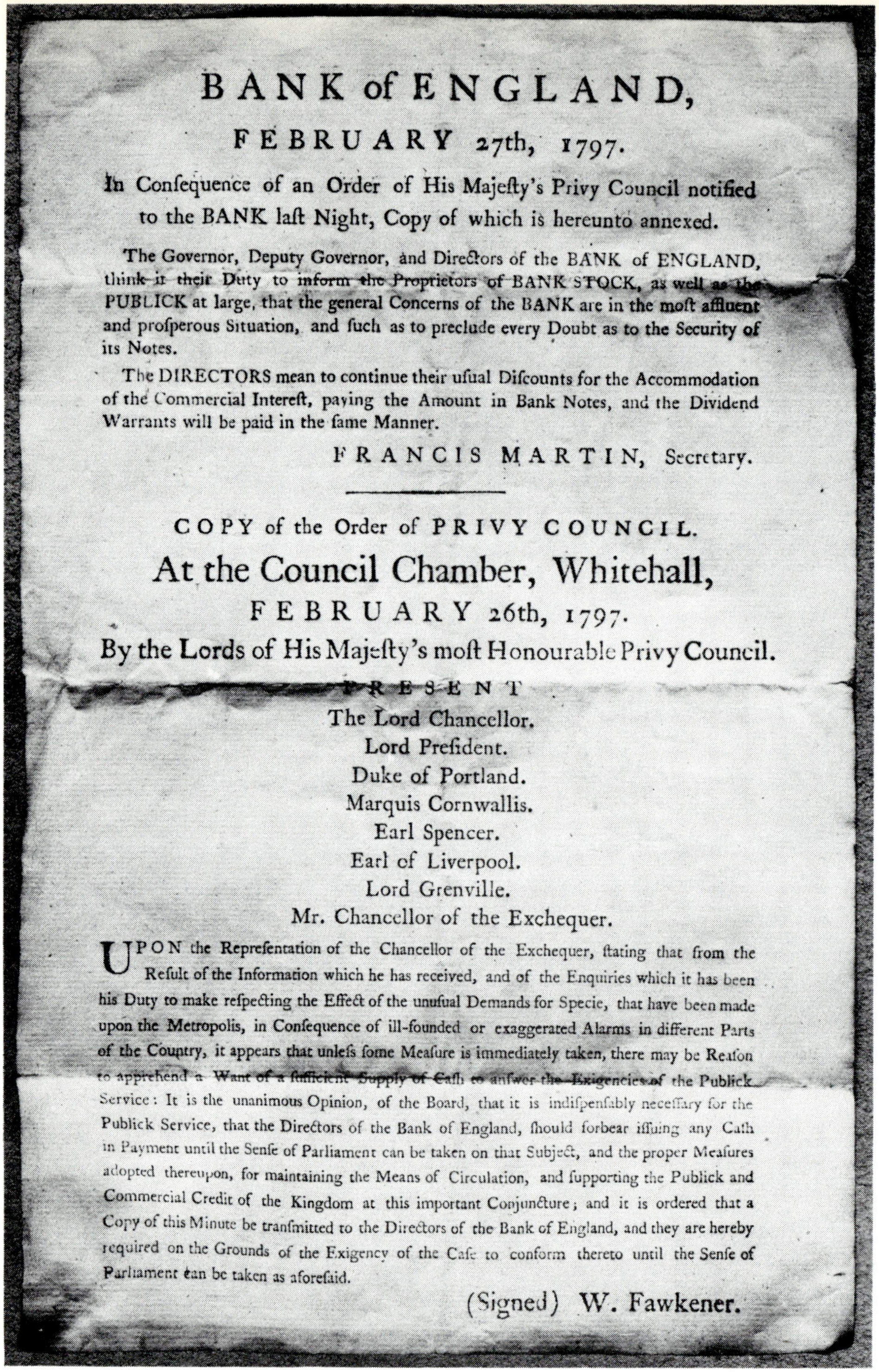

BANK of ENGLAND,

FEBRUARY 27th, 1797.

In Consequence of an Order of His Majesty's Privy Council notified to the BANK last Night, Copy of which is hereunto annexed.

The Governor, Deputy Governor, and Directors of the BANK of ENGLAND, think it their Duty to inform the Proprietors of BANK STOCK, as well as the PUBLICK at large, that the general Concerns of the BANK are in the most affluent and prosperous Situation, and such as to preclude every Doubt as to the Security of its Notes.

The DIRECTORS mean to continue their usual Discounts for the Accommodation of the Commercial Interest, paying the Amount in Bank Notes, and the Dividend Warrants will be paid in the same Manner.

FRANCIS MARTIN, Secretary.

COPY of the Order of PRIVY COUNCIL.

At the Council Chamber, Whitehall,

FEBRUARY 26th, 1797.

By the Lords of His Majesty's most Honourable Privy Council.

PRESENT

The Lord Chancellor.
Lord President.
Duke of Portland.
Marquis Cornwallis.
Earl Spencer.
Earl of Liverpool.
Lord Grenville.
Mr. Chancellor of the Exchequer.

UPON the Representation of the Chancellor of the Exchequer, stating that from the Result of the Information which he has received, and of the Enquiries which it has been his Duty to make respecting the Effect of the unusual Demands for Specie, that have been made upon the Metropolis, in Consequence of ill-founded or exaggerated Alarms in different Parts of the Country, it appears that unless some Measure is immediately taken, there may be Reason to apprehend a Want of a sufficient Supply of Cash to answer the Exigencies of the Publick Service: It is the unanimous Opinion, of the Board, that it is indispensably necessary for the Publick Service, that the Directors of the Bank of England, should forbear issuing any Cash in Payment until the Sense of Parliament can be taken on that Subject, and the proper Measures adopted thereupon, for maintaining the Means of Circulation, and supporting the Publick and Commercial Credit of the Kingdom at this important Conjuncture; and it is ordered that a Copy of this Minute be transmitted to the Directors of the Bank of England, and they are hereby required on the Grounds of the Exigency of the Case to conform thereto until the Sense of Parliament can be taken as aforesaid.

(Signed) W. Fawkener.

67. **Suspension of Payments by the Bank of England**—By this notice on 27 February 1797 the government instructed the Bank of England not to repay in gold its issued notes. The original intention was for a short suspension only but the measure continued for a further 24 years—years in which a long war was fought and won and in which banking, finance and the whole economic life of the country had undergone decisive change.

68. **Bank of England Token Money**—Throughout the eighteenth century the supply of silver currency was hopelessly inadequate. Moreover, newly minted coins were worth more as metal than their face value and it was profitable to melt them down or export them with their consequent loss from circulation. When the Bank of England was forbidden to exchange its notes for gold (67) matters became worse and in 1797 the Bank was authorised to issue the Spanish "pieces of eight" held in its vaults as bullion. At first they carried a small punchmarked head of George III but in 1804 a Boulton and Watt steam press was used to obliterate the Spanish markings and produce a Bank of England dollar. From 1811 to 1816 Bank tokens for 3s. and 1s. 6d. were also issued. In 1817 when the Mint, with up to date machinery was at last able to issue an adequate coinage, these tokens were withdrawn gradually. In nineteen years the Bank had issued £5½ million of token money whereas during the whole of the eighteenth century the Royal Mint issued only £1½ million of silver currency.

69. **George Cruikshank's Bank Restriction Note 1819**—In an age when the death penalty was exacted for offences which would now merit little more than a fine, forgers were hanged and those found guilty of possessing a forged note could be sentenced to transportation for 14 years. In the year 1817, it is said 28,412 forged £1 notes were detected and between 1797 and 1829 618 persons were sentenced to death. In many cases juries refused to convict against the clearest proof and it seems that the Bank of England Directors, bound to prosecute when forgery was detected and vilified by the press of the day, were as sickened by the whole disgusting business as anyone else. In January 1819 Cruikshank was passing the Old Bailey, then the site of Newgate Prison, when he saw a number of bodies hanging from the gibbet. Two of these were women and one had been hung for passing forged pound notes. He went home and in ten minutes designed this horrifying and macabre "Bank Restriction Note"—at first glance a replica of a bank note. It shows the gallows with its string of bodies including the two women. The hangman's rope makes a pound sign surrounding the prison windows crammed with the faces of further victims and Britannia is shown devouring her own children. The signature is that of Jack Ketch, the popular name for the hangman of the day. In 1832 the death penalty for this offence was abolished and transportation for life substituted.

70. **Andrew Drummond of Cadland**—A portrait by Romney of the man described as "marked by a polite seriousness and lack of frivolity" which was less typical of his own times (1755-1833) than those of his twentieth century successors who were to pass the Charing Cross bank to the Royal Bank of Scotland. This purchase marked the beginning of a move into English banking by the Royal Bank which was later to give the National and Commercial Banking Group through its ownership of Williams and Glyn's a substantial fifth place amongst the English Clearing Banks.

71. **George III's letter to Andrew Drummond forwarding his private account book**—When the supporters of Thomas Coutts' son-in-law Sir Francis Burdett marched to Kew Palace and sang revolutionary songs under the old King's windows George III transferred all his accounts to Drummonds, the other Charing Cross bankers. This note from the King asks for his pass book to be written up to date and brought back personally by Andrew Drummond to the Queens Palace—later Buckingham Palace.

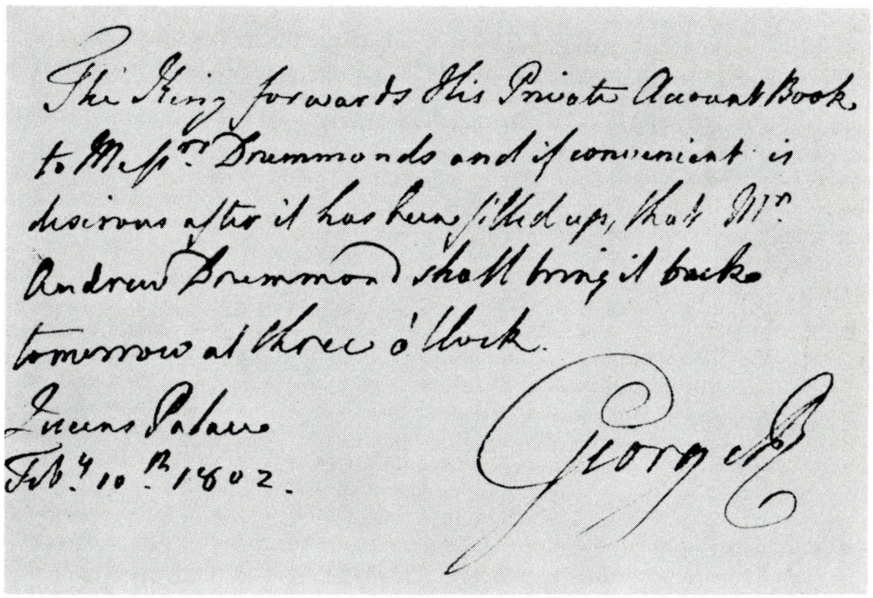

The King forwards His Private Account Book to Mess.rs Drummonds and if convenient is desirous after it has been filled up, that Mr. Andrew Drummond shall bring it back tomorrow at three o'clock.

Queens Palace
Feb.y 10.th 1802.

George R

72A. **Coutts' and Co**—The bank which has traded under the sign of the Three Crowns for almost three centuries traces its foundation to the goldsmith banking partnership of George Middleton and John Campbell in St. Martin's Lane.

72B. **Thomas Coutts**—The Coutts family first became connected with the Three Crowns partnership in 1755, and twenty years later began the long reign of Thomas Coutts, banker and friend of Royalty and statesmen. He made the bank world famous and himself one of the richest and most influential men of his times.

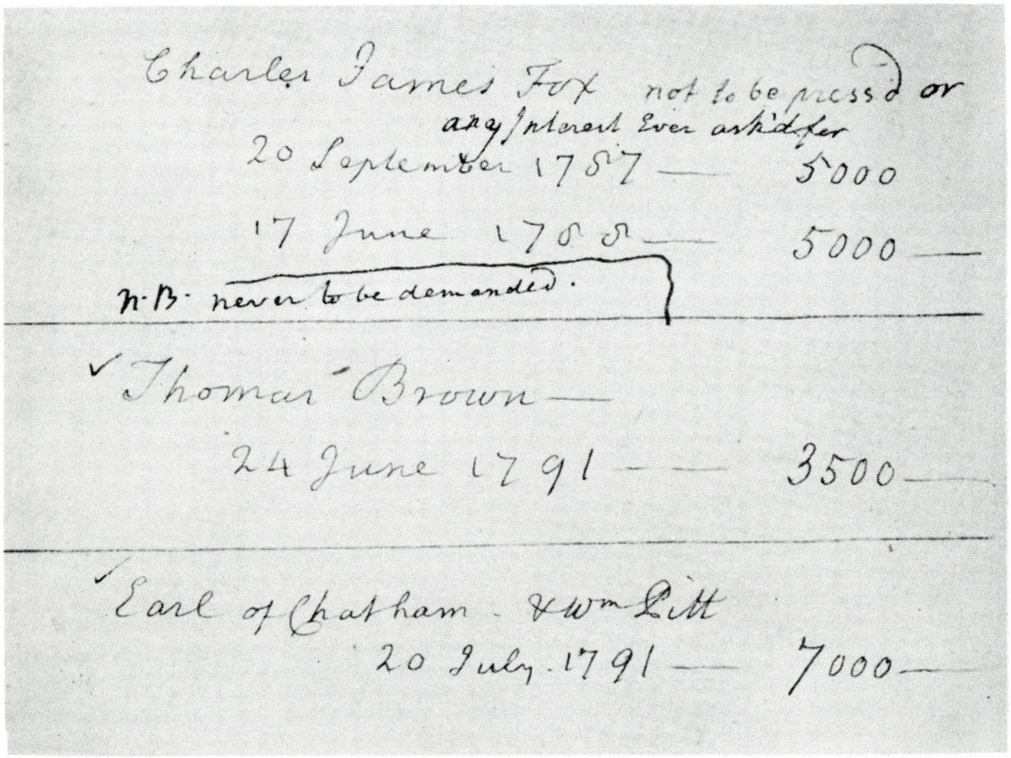

Charles James Fox not to be pressd or
any Interest Ever ask'd for
20 September 1787 — 5000
17 June 1788 — 5000 —
N.B. never to be demanded.

Thomas Brown —
24 June 1791 — 3500 —

Earl of Chatham & Wm Pitt
20 July 1791 — 7000 —

73. **Wm. Pitt the Younger and Charles James Fox**—Thomas Coutts was banker to the two great political contenders of the late eighteenth century. His private notebook shows loans to both. Typical of his relationship with Fox is the original note "not to be pressed" followed by "or any interest asked for" and "N.B. Never to be demanded"—and the final remark on the next sheet—"Worth nothing". Undoubtedly, he fell under the charm of the 'prince of orators' but he knew him also as the close friend of the Prince of Wales, later George IV. Coutts valued his position as banker to the Royal Family, a connection the firm has continued to this day.

74. Licence to Issue Notes, 1810—By the first decade of the nineteenth century well over 700 country banks were in existence—as against the dozen of fifty years previously. Many had developed as an off-shoot of trading or manufacturing and almost all issued their own bank notes. Some of these early banks were well managed and had adequate resources but in times of crisis many failed. In 1808 the government required any person issuing promissory notes to take out a licence and for England and Wales 755 were issued. The Kendal Bank which took out this licence survived the difficulties of the period eventually to form part of the Barclays grouping.

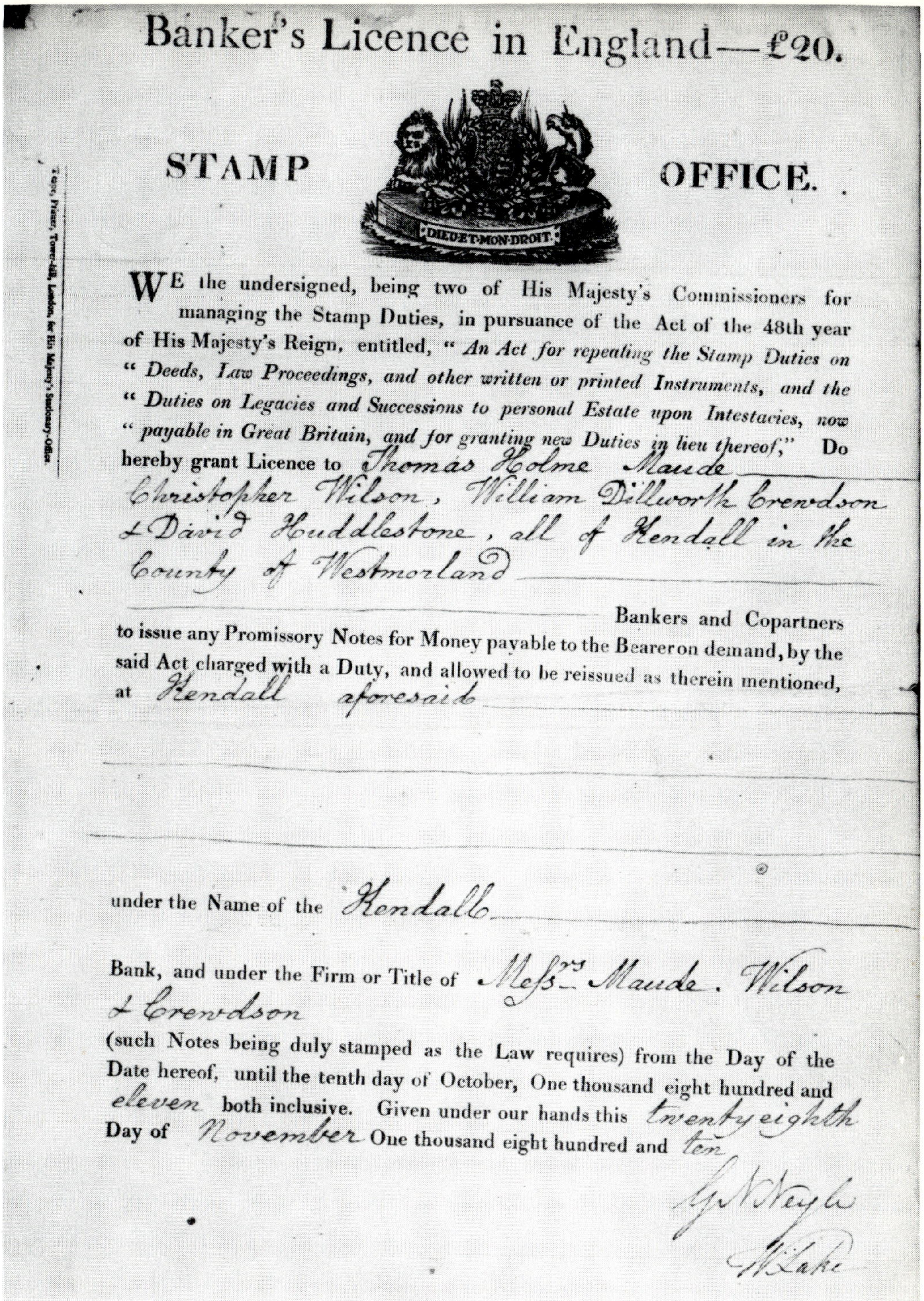

Banker's Licence in England—£20.

STAMP OFFICE.

Tagg, Printer, Tower-hill, London, for His Majesty's Stationery-Office.

WE the undersigned, being two of His Majesty's Commissioners for managing the Stamp Duties, in pursuance of the Act of the 48th year of His Majesty's Reign, entitled, "*An Act for repealing the Stamp Duties on "Deeds, Law Proceedings, and other written or printed Instruments, and the "Duties on Legacies and Successions to personal Estate upon Intestacies, now "payable in Great Britain, and for granting new Duties in lieu thereof,*" Do hereby grant Licence to Thomas Holme Maude Christopher Wilson, William Dillworth Crewdson & David Huddlestone, all of Kendall in the County of Westmorland

Bankers and Copartners to issue any Promissory Notes for Money payable to the Bearer on demand, by the said Act charged with a Duty, and allowed to be reissued as therein mentioned, at Kendall aforesaid

under the Name of the Kendall

Bank, and under the Firm or Title of Messrs. Maude. Wilson & Crewdson

(such Notes being duly stamped as the Law requires) from the Day of the Date hereof, until the tenth day of October, One thousand eight hundred and eleven both inclusive. Given under our hands this twenty eighth Day of November One thousand eight hundred and ten

G. N. Neyle

W. Lake

75. **Dolcoath Mine, Camborne, Cornwall**—A copper mine in west Cornwall in the early nineteenth century, typical of those managed or owned by Gundrys (76) and the Miners' Bank partners (77).

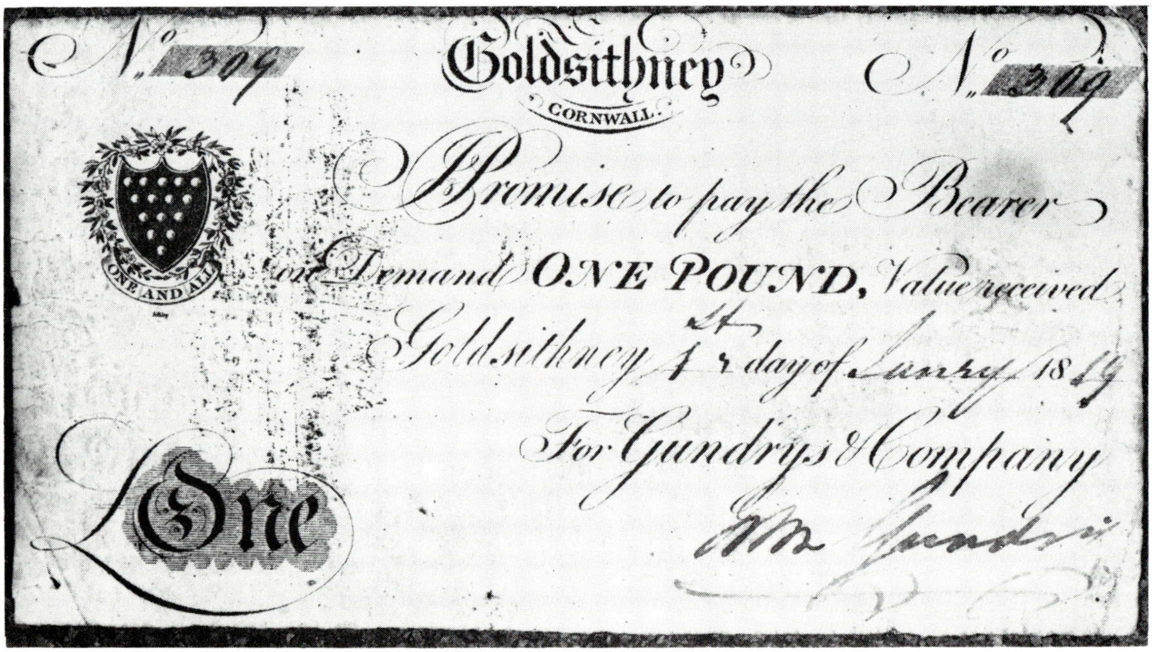

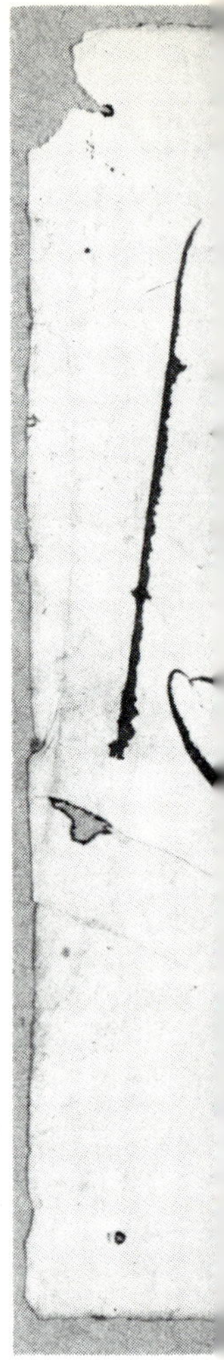

77. **Miners' Bank, Truro £1 Note 1814**—This was one of the earlier country banks with over a hundred years of independent existence before becoming part of the Consolidated Bank of Cornwall, a bank which joined the Barclay grouping in 1905. There is interest in the name marking the many mining customers and the fact that the early partners had widespread interests in the Cornish mining and smelting industries. This full scale illustration shows the size of many early notes.

76. **Gundrys & Company £1 Note**—This note is representative of the many issued by entrepreneurs and others with never any true claim to be bankers. The Cornish coat of arms and motto and the place of issue—Goldsithney—lead us to west Cornwall in the great days of tin and copper mining. The Gundry family—mine managers and owners—were bankrupted in 1819, shortly after the issue of this note. At a time when the supply of currency was scarce, the notes were widely accepted by their workmen and by local suppliers. Many of these old notes survive in Cornwall for who chooses to destroy a bank note?—however remote the possibility of payment.

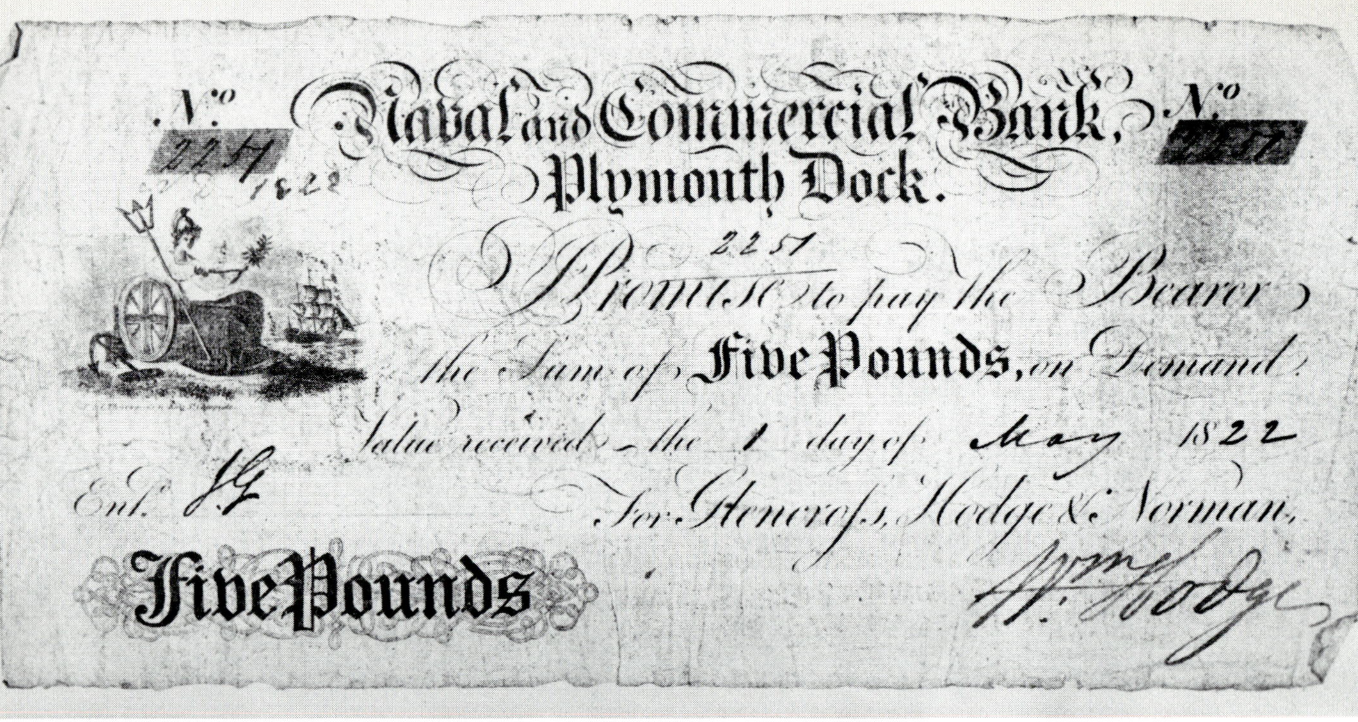
No 2251
1822
Naval and Commercial Bank,
No
Plymouth Dock.
2251
I Promise to pay the Bearer
the Sum of Five Pounds, on Demand.
Value received the 1 day of May 1822
Ent. JG
For Glencross, Hodge & Norman.
Five Pounds
Wm Hodge

78. **Naval and Commercial Bank Note, Plymouth Dock 1822**—Issued when Devonport was known as Plymouth Dock this note displays its birthmark, for all the partners of Glencross, Hodge & Norman were contractors to the Royal Navy as well as bankers.

79. **Devonport Dockyard**—As a main base for the fleet blockading Brest in the Napoleonic Wars, Devonport needed all the supply and financial services offered by the Naval Bank partners.

80. **"Skit" Notes**—Imitation bank notes were issued during the nineteenth century, for propaganda—as with the Cruikshank note (69). They served as advertisements, or to celebrate naval victories or St. Valentine's Day. Sold for a small sum, they raised money for charity but in an illiterate age—and when 700 banks were issuing notes in England and Wales—they could be dangerously like the real thing. The Fort Montague Bank 5 half-pence note was issued by Thomas Hill from his tea house on the River Nidd. His "bank" capital was 13 guineas. On 28 October 1816 the Mayor of Newcastle issued a handbill:—"CAUTION—There are a Set of Swindlers in the Fair attempting to put out as and for Five Pound Notes, certain fictitious notes purporting to issue from the Fort Montague Bank, for the payment of Five Half-pence!!!"

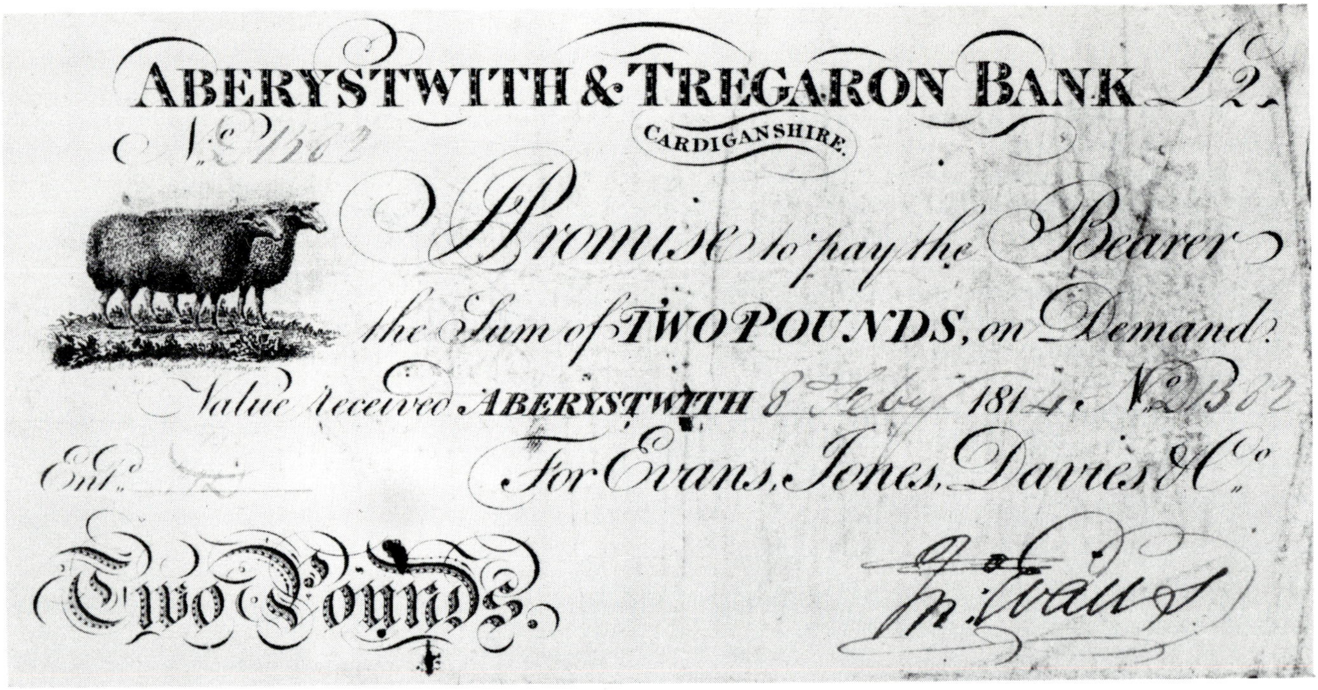
ABERYSTWITH & TREGARON BANK £2
CARDIGANSHIRE
Promise to pay the Bearer
the Sum of TWO POUNDS, on Demand.
Value received ABERYSTWITH 8 Feby 1814
For Evans, Jones, Davies & Co
Two Pounds

85. Stornoway Note 1823—This private issue of notes by J. A. Stewart Mackenzie, the husband of Lady Hood Mackenzie, proprietor of the Island of Lewis, appeared in Stornoway about 1823-26. No bank existed in Stornoway until 1830 and if these notes travelled to the mainland they were paid by the Commercial Bank at Inverness. In the isolated Hebrides, with few ordinary bank notes circulating, this issue would be helpful in providing a local currency.

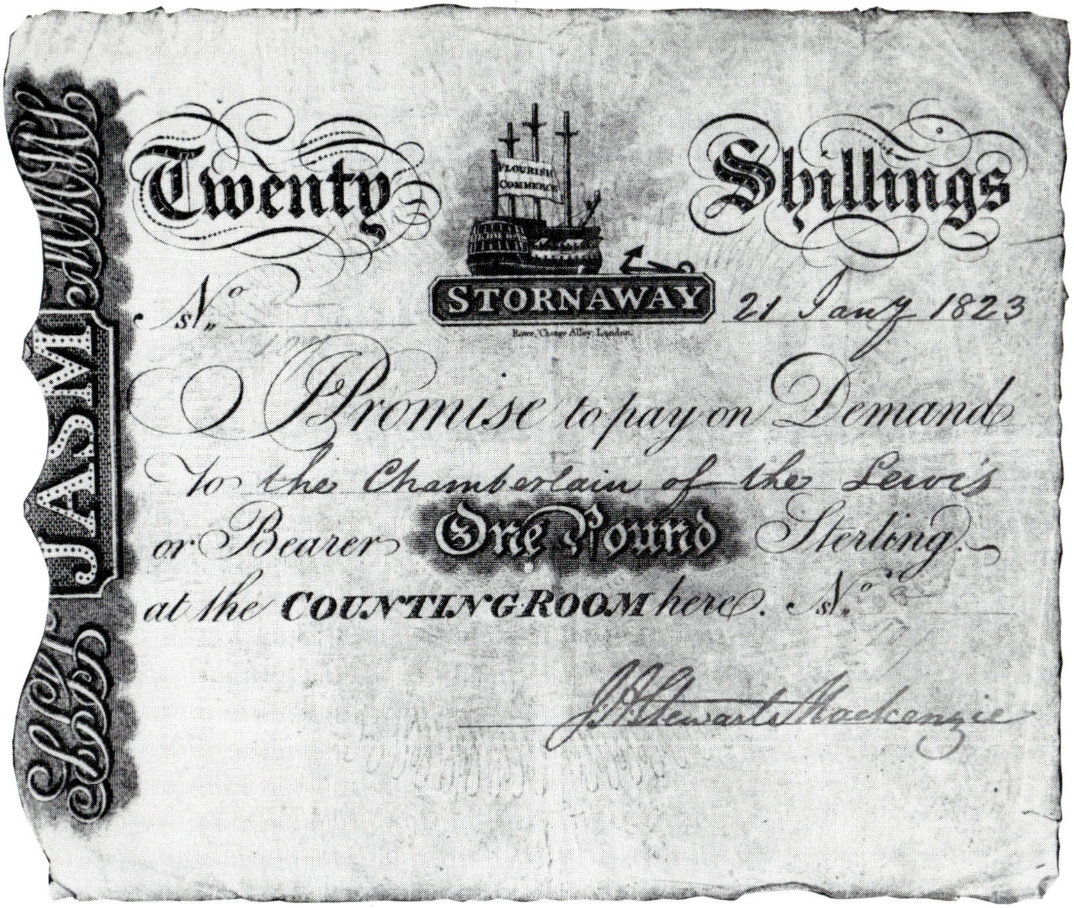

83. The Black Sheep Bank—£2 Note 1814—The Aberystwyth and Tregaron Bank was known locally as "Banc y Ddafad Ddu" because its bank notes carried an engraving of a black sheep. The notes of other banks showed a monogram, a town scene or perhaps a coat of arms. Animals were not unknown but this bank was unusual in varying the number of sheep to match the denomination of the note. This £2 note has two sheep, the £10 note had ten whilst the ten shilling note showed a lamb.

84. Savings Banks—The first savings banks appeared in the early years of the nineteenth century and after a number of attempts to establish semi-charitable organisations the first true savings bank was founded by the Rev. Henry Duncan at Ruthwell, Dumfries-shire, in 1810. An Act of 1817 settled their status and it is from this date that many of the successful Trustee Savings Banks of today trace their foundation. The banks in this period were often run by unpaid volunteers and opened for an hour or two each week to accept small deposits which were taken at some public building. The Corn Exchange, Leicester, was the first office of the Leicester Trustee Savings Bank. When Gladstone established the Post Office Savings Bank in 1861 very many Trustee Savings Banks closed and transferred their depositors to the Post Office. The next half century showed only a modest progress for the surviving Trustee Banks and more rapid expansion for the Post Office—a position which was to be reversed in the following seventy years.

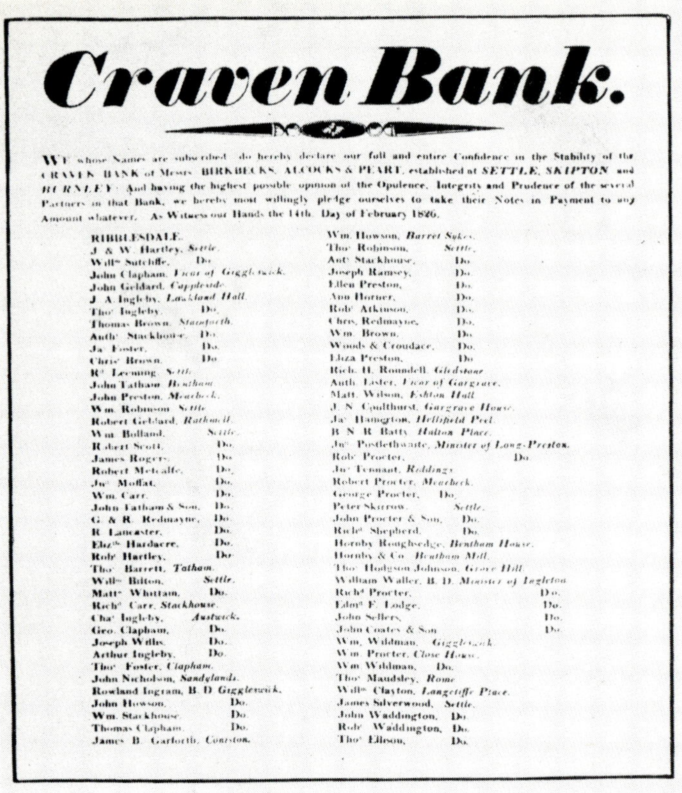

Craven Bank.

WE whose Names are subscribed do hereby declare our full and entire Confidence in the Stability of the CRAVEN BANK of Messrs. BIRKBECKS, ALCOCKS & PEART, established at *SETTLE, SKIPTON* and *BURNLEY*: And having the highest possible opinion of the Opulence, Integrity and Prudence of the several Partners in that Bank, we hereby most willingly pledge ourselves to take their Notes in Payment to any Amount whatever. As Witness our Hands the 14th. Day of February 1826.

RIBBLESDALE.
J. & W. Hartley, *Settle.*
Willm. Sutcliffe, Do.
John Clapham, *Vicar of Giggleswick.*
John Geldard, *Cappleside.*
J. A. Ingleby, *Lawkland Hall.*
Thos. Ingleby, Do.
Thomas Brown, *Stainforth.*
Anthy. Stackhouse, Do.
Jas. Foster, Do.
Chris. Brown, Do.
Rd. Leeming, *Settle.*
John Tatham, *Bentham.*
John Preston, *Meachock.*
Wm. Robinson, *Settle.*
Robert Geldard, *Rathmell.*
Wm. Bolland, *Settle.*
Robert Scott, Do.
James Rogers, Do.
Robert Metcalfe, Do.
Jno. Moffat, Do.
Wm. Carr, Do.
John Tatham & Son, Do.
G. & R. Redmayne, Do.
R. Lancaster, Do.
Elizth. Hardacre, Do.
Robt. Hartley, Do.
Thos. Barrett, *Tatham.*
Willm. Bilton, *Settle.*
Mattw. Whittam, Do.
Richd. Carr, *Stackhouse.*
Chas. Ingleby, *Austwick.*
Geo. Clapham, Do.
Joseph Willis, Do.
Arthur Ingleby, Do.
Thos. Foster, *Clapham.*
John Nicholson, *Sandylands.*
Rowland Ingram, B. D. *Giggleswick.*
John Howson, Do.
Wm. Stackhouse, Do.
Thomas Clapham, Do.
James B. Garforth, *Coniston.*

Wm. Howson, *Barrel Sykes.*
Thos. Robinson, *Settle.*
Anty. Stackhouse, Do.
Joseph Ramsey, Do.
Ellen Preston, Do.
Ann Horner, Do.
Robt. Atkinson, Do.
Chris. Redmayne, Do.
Wm. Brown, Do.
Woods & Croudace, Do.
Eliza Preston, Do.
Rich. H. Roundell, *Gledstone.*
Anth. Lister, *Vicar of Gargrave.*
Matt. Wilson, *Eshton Hall.*
J. N. Coulthurst, *Gargrave House.*
Jas. Hamerton, *Hellifield Peel.*
B. N. R. Batty, *Halton Place.*
Jno. Postlethwaite, *Minister of Long-Preston.*
Robt. Procter, Do.
Jno. Tennant, *Riddings.*
Robert Procter, *Meachock.*
George Procter, Do.
Peter Skirrow, *Settle.*
John Procter & Son, Do.
Richd. Shepherd, Do.
Hornby Roughsedge, *Bentham House.*
Hornby & Co. *Bentham Mill.*
Thos. Hodgson Johnson, *Grove Hill.*
William Waller, B. D. *Minister of Ingleton.*
Richd. Procter, Do.
Edmd. F. Lodge, Do.
John Sellers, Do.
John Coates & Son, Do.
Wm. Wildman, *Giggleswick.*
Wm. Procter, *Close House.*
Wm. Wildman, Do.
Thos. Maudsley, *Rome.*
Willm. Clayton, *Langcliffe Place.*
James Silverwood, *Settle.*
John Waddington, Do.
Robt. Waddington, Do.
Thos. Ellison, Do.

86. **Craven Bank—Declaration of Confidence**—The disastrous late 1825 and early 1826 saw the failure of 60 banks in England and Wales. Since the failure of the local bank always had a serious effect on business it was often the practice of traders and local notables to issue a public notice stating their confidence in the bank partners and offering to accept the bank's notes in payment of any debt due to them. Such a notice could quieten rumours of insolvency and prevent a quite unjustified "run" on a sound bank.

87. **Craven Bank Note, 1821**—Not every bank justified its Declaration of Confidence but this note, issued five years before the bank crisis year and finally paid in 1876, gives proof that the Craven Bank survived the difficult period. Issued for one guinea at Settle it bears the famous Craven heifer. Bred by a customer of the bank the animal reached a great size and many local farmers preferred notes "wi' the cow on" to those of the Bank of England.

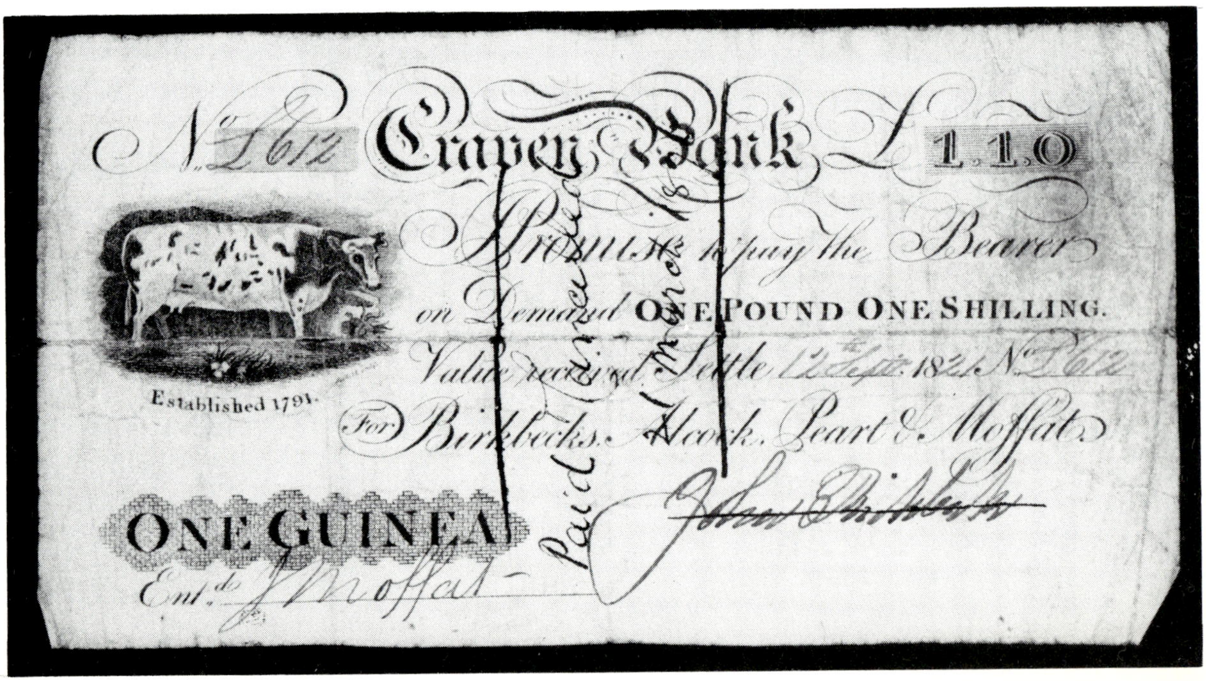

88. **The Stoppage of The Bank**—Bristol artist Rolinda Sharples chose this subject since she considered "suspension of payment at a bank, as well suited to a great variety of expression". Completed very shortly after the crisis year of 1825-1826, the buildings in the background are typical of Bristol. Although she must have had in mind the failure of the Bristol Bullion Bank in December 1825, the picture could depict any of the anxious groups of ordinary people who assembled up and down the country—waiting, pass book in hand—but with little hope that their bank would re-open its doors to repay their savings.

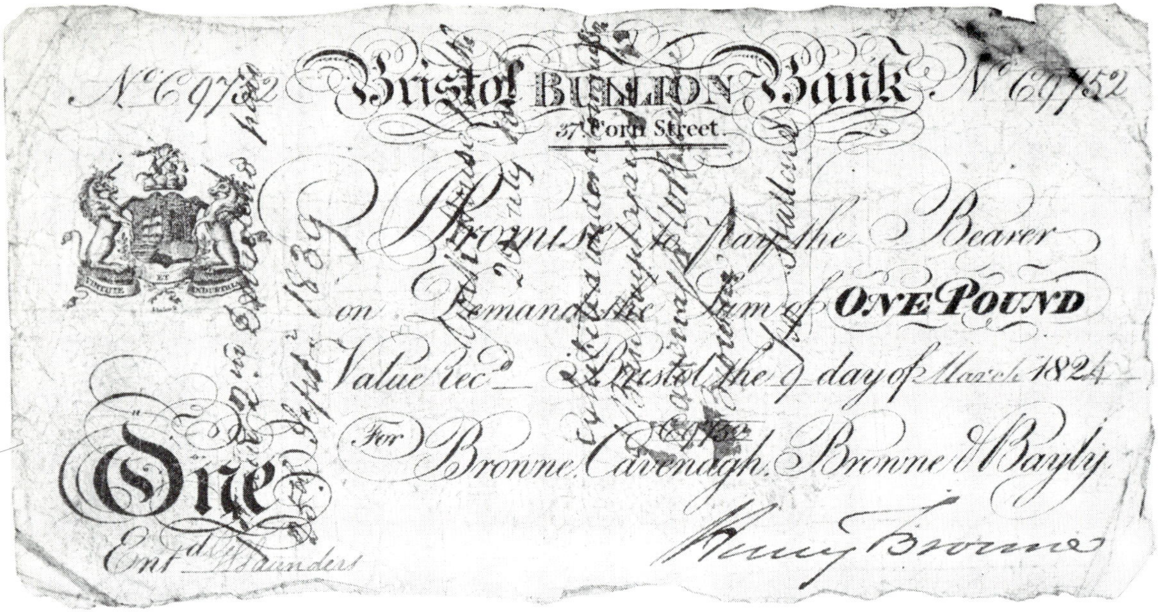

89. **Bristol Bullion Bank note 1825—** Issued a few months before this Bristol bank failed on December 20 1825. The note is stamped as evidence of production for payment of two bankruptcy dividends for the quite substantial total of 13s.4d. in the pound.

91. **Stuckey's Bristol and Somersetshire Bank**—During the latter part of the eighteenth and for much of the nineteenth century cheques and bank post bills, drawn by a country banker on his London agent, were a popular way to remit money. They were issued in exchange for cash and payable to the person named by the purchaser. Being drawn for payment a number of days after sight—or as in this case after date—there was ample time to ensure they were not paid even if stolen in post.

90. **The Queen's Dolls House pass book**—The pass books held by the waiting crowd in the Rolinda Sharples picture (88) show that the old practice of calling at the bank, inspecting the ledger and signing it as correct (33) had been replaced by a pass book giving a copy of the account. This kind of passbook is no longer in use but here is a perfect miniature less than the size of a farthing—or a decimal penny. Showing the Queen's Dolls House Account with the National Provincial Bank, it forms part of the exhibit at Windsor Castle.

92. **Banbury Old Bank and Advertisement**—Until comparatively recent times bankers have made little use of advertising. With a modest announcement in the Public Notices column of a local newspaper a new bank would open for business, or perhaps a paragraph would note a centenary. This card of the 1820's is sober in layout but gives the same message as the colourful full page newspaper advertisements of the present day Lloyds Bank of which the Banbury Old Bank became a part.

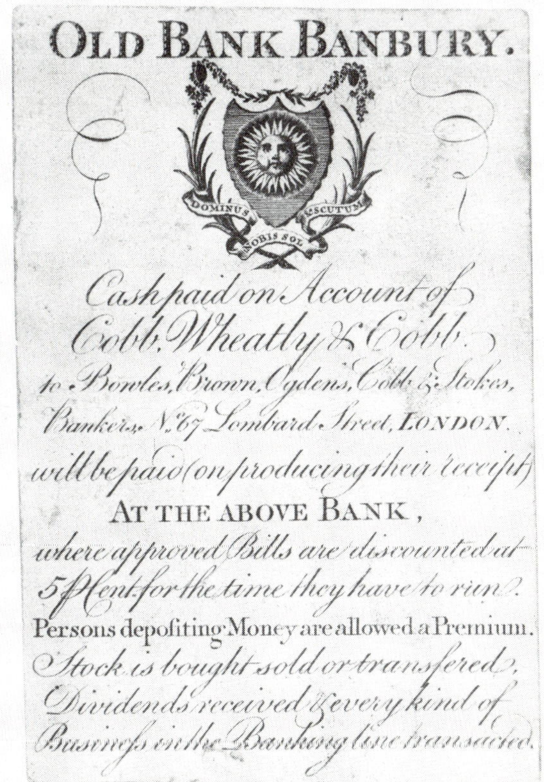

93. **Transfer Day at the Bank of England 1836**—The horrific "skit" note (69) showed George Cruikshank, artist and illustrator of Charles Dickens' novels, as a social and political caricaturist but much of his work was in a lighter vein. Here he depicts one of the Stock Transfer Offices at the Bank of England with pickpockets at work and a police officer complete with handcuffs about to make an arrest.

94. **Watermark Press**—Forgery of bank notes of the Bank of England and the country banks was always a matter for concern. When the Bank of England asked the public for suggestions to improve their notes nearly 400 were received. One was to change the straight lines of the old watermark to waved lines and to incorporate in the watermark the denomination of the note. The forger soon found the means to defeat the precautions and this small metal on wood press was used for forging the watermark on Bank of England notes.

95. **Joint Stock Banking and the National Provincial Bank of England**—Alarmed by the failures of 1826 and impressed by the relative stability of the Scottish joint stock banks, with their large number of shareholders and spread of branches, the government intervened. An Act of 1826 allowed banking partnerships of any number of members to be formed if more than 65 miles from London, the latter a provision intended to protect the Bank of England. The first of these new joint stock banks was the Lancaster Banking Company in 1827 and within ten years there were a hundred such banks in operation. Many were smaller than the private banks with which they were competing and it was the later Bank Charter Act of 1833 which made possible the growth of the great commercial banks of the twentieth century with their vast resources and 12,000 branches. The London and Westminster Bank opening for business on 10 March 1834 was narrowly beaten for first place by the National Provincial Bank of England which opened its first office in King Street, Gloucester, on January 1. Within a few years the business was transferred to these premises in Westgate Street. In 1968 the Westminster and National Provincial Banks amalgamated to make the largest bank in the United Kingdom.

96. **City Bank Charter**—Until 1857 every new joint stock bank was required to obtain a Royal Charter. In effect the birth certificate of the bank, it was an impressive document as is shown by this 1855 charter for the City Bank.

97. **Aerial View of the Bank of England**—By the mid-nineteenth century the Bank of England buildings had reached the form they were to retain until the 1930's. This early aerial photograph shows the jumble of buildings and courtyards within a curtain wall which made up the old Bank. Also can be picked out the Head Office sites of three of the modern "big four" Clearing Banks, the Royal Exchange and the Mansion House. The outline of the Bank's first buildings can be clearly traced (37).

99. **A Banker's Locked Book**—In a period when all letters were written by hand, copies of confidential letters and information regarding customers were kept in locked books to which only the partners or manager had access.

98. **The Bankers' Clearing House 1847**—At this date the Clearing House was still the preserve of the London private banks whose clerks had originally come together at the "Five Bells" chop house in Dove Court (51). The growing London joint stock banks, the Bank of England and banks outside London were not all to be included until 1864. Looking even further ahead to the 1970's, over 3,000,000 cheques with a value of more than £4,000 million, together with vast numbers of credit items, would be handled in a single day. A similar system dating from 1892 was to be applied to the banks in Scotland, giving Britain one of the most sophisticated and efficient money transfer systems in the world.

100. **Bank Staff**—In 1842 *Punch* described bank clerks as "the hardest worked, worst paid and most polite body of men in the Metropolis". These advertisements in the *Bankers' Magazine* for 1878 reveal a mobility of banking labour which was largely to disappear in the twentieth century. Plainly this was a period when employees were seeking employers and not the reverse as it came to be a hundred years later. In the 1840's even the Bank of England appears to have had staff problems since it was announced "that the Authorities had seen a disposition upon the part of certain Bank clerks to wear moustaches; that they strongly disapproved of the practice, and that if this hint be not attended to, measures will be resorted to which may prove of a painful nature". Record does not not show what the sanctions were to be!

Advertisements.

A CASHIER in one of the leading Irish Banks wishes for a similar appointment in a Country Bank in England.—Highest possible references given: Salary required, £120 per annum.—Address, "C.," office of B. M., 27, Great Winchester Street, London, E.C.

A GENTLEMAN, of ten years' experience in one of the leading Provincial Joint Stock Banks, is desirous of meeting with a re-engagement.—Address, "E.," care of Editor *Bankers' Magazine*, 27, Great Winchester Street, London, E.C.

A GENTLEMAN, who has had 8 years' varied experience in Banking, wishes to take the Management of a Country, Branch Bank. He is able to give testimonials from his present Employers and from other Bankers.—Apply "U.B.," *Bankers' Magazine* Office, 25, Great Winchester Street, E.C.

A GENTLEMAN (25) with five years' varied Banking experience, seeks Re-engagement. Good writer, accurate in figures. First class references from ast employers.—To "Z.," Providence Cottage, Braughing, Ware.

BANK MANAGER.—A Bank Manager of some considerable and successful experience in Country Banking, seeks an appointment as Branch Manager, or Inspector of Branches. Age, 45.—"Moneta," care of Publishers *Bankers' Magazine*, 26, Great Winchester Street, London, E.C.

£50 to anyone procuring a Banking appointment for a Gentleman, aged 28. He was 3 years in a Bank, and has other Financial experience. Highest references. Communications confidential.—Address "A.," 4, Hornsey Street, Holloway, London, N.

TO BANKERS AND OTHERS.—Wanted by a Gentleman thoroughly experienced in Banking Office duties, a clerkship.—Salary, £120.—Bank references. Address, "Trust," care of *Bankers' Magazine*, 27, Great Winchester Street, E.C.

TO BANKERS.—Wanted by a Bank Clerk (24) a re-engagement. Seven years' business experience, three with present employers.—Salary to commence at £100. -Address, "E. A. T." Stamford, Spalding and Boston Banking Company, Boston, Lincolnshire.

WANTED—Appointment as Manager, Sub-Manager, or Branch Manager in a Country Bank. Age 34. 18 years' comprehensive experience, including management and inspection. Unexceptional references and securities. Salary £300—or equivalent. Address, "M. A.," *Bankers' Magazine* 25, Great Winchester Street, E.C.

101. **The Bank Garden**—Passing the smoke blackened walls of the Bank of England in Victorian London who could have realised that behind lay this tree-shaded garden. When, after the Gordon Riots in 1780, the Bank bought the church of St. Christopher-le-Stocks, it agreed to keep the graveyard, which became this garden, as an open space for ever. The garden shows clearly in the aerial photograph (97) and only in the rebuilding of the 1930's was it replaced by a garden court in the heart of the new building. The statue of St. Christopher forms the Bank's War Memorial and commemorates the church which stood on the site.

102. **Head office of the new London and Westminster Bank 1838**—This illustration is of particular interest in showing the first Head Office of a new joint stock bank to be built in London and also the first intrusion of massive commercial architecture into a scale still Georgian and largely domestic. In the neighbouring properties the senior partner of a banking house and some of his unmarried clerks would live over the "shop" and even the goldsmith banker of the seventeenth century would have found familiar surroundings. The later Victorian rebuilding swept away the Georgian City only itself to give way to the steel and concrete multi-storey office blocks of today.

103. **Pay Office of the London and Westminster Bank**—An engraving of 1845 showing the inside of the Lothbury office. Just as the exterior set a style for bank architecture down to the 1930's, this interior was to be a familiar pattern for the next hundred years.

104. **Charles Geach rides for the military**—Each of the great joint stock banks founded in the 1830's can recall a man whose energy and imagination put the bank on the long road to national importance. The Midland owes much to Charles Geach, the former Bank of England clerk who in 1836 at the age of 28 became manager of the newly formed Birmingham and Midland Bank. This was the parent of the present day Midland Bank which still bears the regional name denoting its birthplace. Charles Geach's early years with the new bank were eventful enough and it is recorded that in 1839 he mounted his staff on the roof of the bank, armed with stones and bricks to repel a Chartist mob, and rode his horse through a hail of missiles to fetch help from the barracks.